MW00466267

A Treatise of Earthly-Mindedness

Showing the Great Sin of
Thinking as the World Thinks Rather Than
Thinking God's Thoughts After Him

plus

Conversing in Heaven
and # Walking with God

by JEREMIAH BURROUGHS

Edited by Don Kistler

Soli Deo Gloria Publications
An imprint of Reformation Heritage Books
Grand Rapids, Michigan

Soli Deo Gloria Publications
An imprint of Reformation Heritage Books
3070 29th St. SE
Grand Rapids, MI 49512
616-977-0889
e-mail: orders@heritagebooks.org
website: www.heritagebooks.org

Paperback reprint 2022

ISBN 978-1-60178-966-2

The Library of Congress has cataloged the hardcover
edition as follows:

Burroughs, Jeremiah, 1599-1646.
  [Two treatises of Mr. Jeremiah Burroughs]
  A treatise of earthly-mindedness : showing the great sin of thinking
as the world thinks rather than thinking God's thoughts after him ;
and, A treatise of conversing in heaven and walking with God / by
Jeremiah Burroughs ; edited by Don Kistler. – 1st modern ed.
      p. cm.
  Includes bibliographical references and index.
  ISBN 1-877611-38-7 (alk. paper)
  1. Christian life–Congregational authors. 2. Worldliness. I.
Kistler, Don. II. Burroughs, Jeremiah, 1599-1646. Treatise of
conversing in heaven and walking with God. III. Title. IV. Title:
Treatise of conversing in heaven and walking with God.

BV4501.3.B88 2006
248.4'859–dc22

2005021264

TABLE OF CONTENTS

A Treatise of Earthly-Mindedness

A Heavenly Conversation

Walking with God

FOREWORD TO THE 20TH CENTURY
EDITION OF

A Treatise of Earthly-Mindedness

My guess is that few people will ever pick up this book and read it. Its theme and content are too alien to modern Christianity to evoke much interest.

Twentieth-century Christians have been seduced by a worldview that makes the thrust of this book seem archaic. It simply doesn't fit our times. It's not so much that the contemporary Christian has consciously embraced worldliness, it's more that we have been so influenced by a manner of viewing the world that anything *beyond* this world seems obscured by eclipse.

Gone is a vital sense of Providence. The world is seen as operating according to its internal mechanistic laws. The hand of Providence is not so much regarded as being invisible; it has been erased altogether.

Gone is the blessed hope of heaven. Though interest abounds in the return of Jesus, the contemplation of heaven itself has been banished from our thinking. Our thinking is earth-bound, trapped within the confines of the terrestrial horizon.

Gone is the Biblical doctrine of the soul. There is much concern about self-image, self-esteem, and self-gratification. Yet, in all this, the "self" itself has become a philosophical conundrum. Since Immanuel Kant assigned the "self" to the unknowable noumenal realm, along with God and metaphysical essences, the soul as the core of human selfhood has drifted into intellectual limbo.

Yet it is the human soul that stands to be nourished and fed by this book. Our gaze is lifted beyond the earth, our hearts are set aflame by the fire of heaven, and our minds are awakened to a spiritual perspective.

This volume may be the most comprehensive treatment of the nature and enticements of worldliness. It is a prose version of Bunyan's *Pilgrim's Progress,* reflecting the keen insight of Puritan Christianity. It is far too valuable to be ignored.

R.C. Sproul
Orlando, FL

To the Reader

*I*t was the saying of a servant of Christ, "Every day a Christian spends on earth is a day lost in heaven." He meant it of the place, not the company—for what makes heaven to be heaven but union and communion with God in Jesus Christ? This being attainable in this life, what keeps a Christian from living in heaven while he lives upon earth? Truly our fellowship is with the Father and with His Son Jesus Christ (1 John 1:3). Our conversation is in heaven, said another apostle in Philippians 3:20. "And I live, yet not I, but Christ liveth in me; and the life which I now live in the flesh, I live by the faith of the Son of God" (Galatians 2:20).

These were men on the earth, subject to infirmities as we are, yet living in heaven. And there are yet in this declining, wanton, Christ-denying age, a generation upon earth thus living whose lives and graces, though hidden under a mean outside, under many reproaches and infirmities, yet shine inwardly with the glory of Christ upon them; who, though they are in the world, yet follow the Lord with a different spirit than the spirit of the world. And among these hidden ones of the Lord, this blessed man (the preacher of these sermons, of whom the world was not worthy) was such a one who, while he was upon earth, lived in heaven. And as you may easily perceive, the end and scope of these sermons is to wind up your heart to a like frame and posture, that is, to take it off of perishing vanities and to set it on that which is the real and durable substance.

We see upon what weak shoulders the fair neck of all worldly pomp and glory now stands, and how the Lord is winding up and putting an end to the glories of the kingdoms of men who have not contributed their strength and power to the advancing, but rather to the pulling down and eclipsing of the glory of the kingdom of Jesus Christ. Besides what the world tells us, never has an age had more examples laid before them of the world's vanity than in our days. Therefore, our hearts should sit loose to all things that cannot stretch themselves to eternity. The apostle's reason is full of weight:

> It remains that both they that have wives be as though they had none; and they that weep as though they wept not; and they that rejoiced as though they rejoiced not; and they that buy as though they possessed not; and they that use the world as not abusing it.

And this exhortation he puts on by this argument: "The time is short," or, as the word is, "the remainder of our season is now folding up, as a veil or curtain into a narrow room."

Time is short and life is shorter, and the end of all things is at hand. We have greater things to mind and to set our hearts upon. The divinity of this holy man's spirit much appeared in this, that having much of the comfort that earth could afford him, he still looked upon all creature contentments with the eyes of a stranger, and in order to the raising of his soul to a more holy, humble, serviceable, self-denying walking with God. For a man who enjoys little or nothing in this world to speak much of the world's vanity and emptiness, and of taking the heart off that, is not as much as when a man is surrounded with the confluence of creature comforts then, by a Divine spirit, to tread upon the neck of these things, and to be caught up into the third Heaven, bathing, solacing, and satisfying itself with sweet and higher enjoyments, with the more savory and cordial apprehensions it has of Jesus Christ. This is comparable to the one who is made a partaker of the Divine nature, and who lives above the world in the enjoyment of the world.

So now, reader, you have these sermons twice printed: once in the practice of this holy man and once again in these papers which we present to you in this preaching style (though we confess things might have been more contracted) because we find this more desired, more acceptable to his hearers and, if we mistake not, more working upon the affections and more profitable to the greatest number of Christians.

The Lord Jesus be with your spirit, and go along with these, and all his other precious labors, to the furtherance of the joy of your faith, building you up in the inner man, and directing you in the way to your eternal rest.

Thomas Goodwin	*William Bridge*
William Greenhill	*William Adderly*
John Yates	*Sydrach Simpson*
Philip Nye	

A Treatise of Earthly-Mindedness

". . . who mind earthly things. . . "

PHILIPPIANS 3:19

CHAPTER ONE

The Text Opened

"*. . . who mind earthly things. . .* "

PHILIPPIANS 3:19

This precious Scripture clearly holds forth the different dispositions of wicked and of godly men, especially of such wicked men as set themselves against the gospel, for it relates to such as were professed enemies to the cross of Christ, that labored as best they could to hinder the success of the ministry of Paul. You will find, if you look back a few verses, that this is meant of that kind of men especially, for he tells us that many walked so, as they were enemies to the cross of Christ. They were those that opposed the preaching of Paul and his ministry. He describes those men by divers characteristics; but I'll treat none of them but this one: "who mind earthly things," who savor or relish earthly things (you may translate either as well). It is a general word comprehending the actions and operations of both the understanding and the will. It is, in Scripture, applied to both, but most commonly to the actions of the will and affections. We will deal particularly with actions of the will.

Earthly things are those that are on the earth, whatever they are, the beauty, the glory, and pageantry of the earth; the profits that are earthly, the pleasures and honors of the world; who mind any things inordinately that are sublunary accommodations. But we carry and behave ourselves as free denizens of the city of heaven, for so the words in the original are, if we should thus read them, "Our city, where we are citizens and where we have rights, is heaven."

But our conversation, our city converse, is of things that are above the earth. When the apostle would have men to follow his example and not the example of others, in the 17th verse, he uses this as an argument that such and such men are enemies to the cross of Christ, and they make their belly their god, and they mind earthly things. Do not follow them; do not hearken what they say to you; they come up and down from house to house and whisper this and that to you, and would take you off from the ways of God. God has begun to enlighten you and to stir your consciences; do not let the precious affections of your souls run toward them, but be followers of us as we are of Christ, for our conversation is in heaven with our Lord and Master, this argument coming in the 20th verse. That being the only scope and meaning of the words, take this doctrinal truth:

DOCTRINE: The great difference between a wicked man and a godly man is that one minds earthly things and the other has his conversation in heaven. I intend to handle both these in order.

One of these minds earthly things. It is a parallel Scripture to Romans 8:5, for they that are after the flesh do mind the things of the flesh. "Do mind," there is the same word, only here it is the participle and there it is the verb, but the meaning is the same. They that are after the earth mind earthly things; they that are after the flesh favor fleshly things. The first part of this point is the description of wicked men, they that are enemies to the cross of Christ and to the ways of godliness. They are men that mind earthly things, and the more gross of them are described before this as having their bellies as their gods. Some of them are very sensual, drunken, unclean, and altogether given to satisfy the flesh in fleshly lusts. But there are others that do not appear to be so brutish, yet they are men of earthly minds who savor only earthly things, and these are the men that are secret enemies to the cross of Christ, yea, and will many times appear so to be; it will break out at length. Such a man whose spirit has been earthly for a long time will appear at length to be an enemy to Christ's cross. Now in the handling of this point, I will propound these five things:

First, what it is to mind earthly things in a sinful way, or thus: When a man may be said to be an earthly-minded man, that we may know when a man is an earthly-minded man, what it is to mind earthly things that the apostle describes here a wicked man by. Without the opening of this, all that I shall say afterwards will be to little purpose.

Second, the great evil that there is in minding earthly things, and I shall help you discover a greater evil in it than you are aware of.

Third, lay down some proofs whereby those men and women that think they are clear of this sin may have it revealed to their consciences that they are the men and women that do mind earthly things.

Fourth, I shall search into the reason why the hearts of men and women are so much after earthly things.

Fifth, I shall labor to take your hearts off of earthly things. These are the five things that are to be done in the first part of the point, namely, the character of wicked men here laid down, who mind earthly things.

First, who they are who mind earthly things. Certainly they are not all those that enjoy earthly things. All men who make use of earthly things must not be condemned for minding them. Paul himself, in this very epistle (Philippians 4:12), wrote that though he knew how to want, yet he knew how to abound. He could tell how to make use of earthly things, and he gives charge that all those that are instructed should make such as had instructed them partakers of all their goods. Paul charges this! Yea, Christ Himself, in that Scripture where He labors most to take the thoughts of men off the earth, and not to take any thought for what they should eat or drink, still says, "Your heavenly Father knows that ye have need of these things" (Matthew 6:32). Galatians 6:6: "Let him that is taught in the Word communicate unto him that teacheth all good things." And if there is any pretence against it, yet he says, "Be not deceived, God is not mocked; for whatsoever a man soweth, that shall he also reap." Therefore, it is not here charged, as a mark of an evil man, to have earthly things, and to justly require what is due unto him, as Paul does here. And the Galatians could not charge him with breaking his own rule that he wrote to the Philippians. Therefore, we must inquire what is meant by "minding earthly things." When does a man or woman mind earthly things in a sinful way? For that there are several particulars.

CHAPTER TWO

Earthly-Mindedness Discovered in Nine Particulars

1. A man is earthly-minded when he looks upon earthly things as the greatest things of all, when he has a high esteem of earthly things as the things. As if it were thus: "Oh, if I had such and such things as others have, oh, how happy I would be! How happy are such and such men that do enjoy such earthly things at their will, in their dwellings, their furniture, their comings in; oh, these are the excellent things, these are the delightful things. These are the things in which felicity and happiness consist."

When men promise themselves felicity in any earthly things, they mind earthly things. I remember golden-mouthed Chrysostom had a speech about a covetous man who looked upon his money and saw more beauty in his money than in the very sun that shines in the firmament. Men look upon the things of the earth as the most beautiful things in their eyes. Certainly a man is in a distemper when he puts such a high esteem upon any earthly things. This esteem is not according to what God and His saints put upon earthly things. God never puts any great eminency on any earthly thing. He never made any earthly things to be any great conduit or means of conveyance of any great good from Himself unto His creature. If you would know where your heart is, you may know it by this one sign as much as any: what do you count your excellency? According to what any man or woman counts their excellency to consist in, so is their heart. Their hearts are suitable.

In Genesis 27:28–39, you find Isaac blessing Jacob and Esau. But I would have you observe the difference in the placement of them. Observe the blessing of Jacob in verse 28. There God gives the dew of heaven and the fatness of the earth, and plenty of corn and wine as Jacob's blessing. Now look at Esau's blessing, for the blessing was suitable to their disposition. Jacob's father answered and said unto him, "Behold thy dwelling shall be of the fatness of the earth, and of the dew of heaven from above." Mark it, Isaac blessed them both with the dew of heaven and fatness of the earth. But in Jacob's blessing the dew of heaven was first and the fatness of the earth was second; while in Esau's blessing, the fatness of the earth was first and then the dew of heaven. Note that a godly man stands in need of earthly things. As Christ said, "Your Father knows you stand in need of these things." But the great thing, in the first place, that a godly heart minds is the dew of heaven, and then second the blessing of the earth. Now a carnal heart thinks that it has some need of the things of heaven; it will acknowledge that. But it's the fatness of the earth they desire, and then the dew of heaven.

So that's the first thing: earthly-minded men look upon these things as the high and chief things; and hence it is that the choice thoughts of an earthly-minded man are carried out on worldly objects.

2. When the creamy, choice thoughts of men and women are busied about earthly things, they mind earthly things in a sinful manner. You may know what kind of hearts you have by

your thoughts about anything. The thoughts are the immediate ebullitions or risings up of the heart, that is, the bubbles that come from the heart immediately.

A man cannot know what is in his heart as much by words and actions as by the thoughts, because the thoughts immediately spring from the heart. For example, I can tell what the water is in such a fountain better from that which bubbles up immediately from the fountainhead than I can tell by the water that runs in the stream a mile or two off that never came from the fountainhead. That which immediately bubbles from the fountainhead reveals the nature of the fountain.

The thoughts are, as it were, the firstborn of the heart; and therefore the heart may be known by the thoughts. The Holy Ghost said in Proverbs 23:7, "As a man thinketh in his heart, so is he." That which is here spoken in particular may be applied in general. As a man thinks in his heart, so is he; as his thoughts are, so is he. The heart is as the thoughts of the mind are. Men may keep words in and actions out by respects. If you could know what the heart is and look into the haunts of it in secret, it would reveal to you what you are. Many of your servants, when in your presence or before others, may, out of respect, carry themselves fairly. But if you would find them out, labor to know what they do when they are alone in their private haunts.

So, would you know your own hearts? Do not look so much at them and take a scantling of them by how you behave yourselves in words and actions before others, but what they are in your private chambers, what they are in the inward thoughts of the mind; there the heart comes to be discovered most. By these thoughts I do not mean every kind of injection or suggestion, for sometimes the devil may cast evil thoughts into the most holy. But I mean such thoughts as are sweet to the soul, whereby the soul comes to suck out sweetness and contentment, for that's minding earthly things: when you find the strength of your thoughts to be upon the things of the earth, and they are more suitable to your hearts than any other. It is not when through weakness the mind may be wandering this way or that way, or through suggestions or temptations; but men or women are most themselves when alone and free. Can you say when you are alone, "Oh, the very thoughts of God are sweet to me! I meditate in His law day and night." Can you suck out sweetness there as from a honeycomb? But an unclean wretch will suck sweetness out of his unclean thoughts when he is alone. The earthly-minded man will suck sweetness out of his earthly thoughts, and the ambitious man the sweetness of his pride when he is alone; and these are the most contentful thoughts to him. He can run two or three hours and take delight and pleasure in them—that's earthly-mindedness.

3. An earthly-minded man is one whose heart cleaves to the earth. As I told you, the word was not only to mind, but to savor the things of the earth; his heart cleaves to the earth. The Psalmist, in a far different case, said that his soul cleaved to the dust; but that's true of many men in this case. Their very souls cleave to the dust; their spirits are mixed with the earth, and therefore they are dross. It may be they have some good common gifts, some good natural parts, and some workings of the Holy Ghost upon them; yet their spirits are drossy because they are mixed with the earth. Talk to these men of the vanity of the things of the earth. They will give you a hearing, but when you have done all their souls cleave to the earth. And talk to them of the excellency of heavenly things. They will hear you, but when you have done all their souls still cleave to the earth, as a man whose soul cleaves in love to a woman (as it is said of Samson, his soul cleaved to Delilah). Say what you will against that woman, or of the excellency of any other woman, yet his soul

cleaves to that woman.

So it is in an earthly-minded man: let what will be said against the things of the earth, or what can be said for setting forth the excellency of the things of heaven, yet his soul cleaves to the earth as the serpent's belly did to the dust of the ground. That's an earthly-minded man.

4. An earthly-minded man is one whose heart is filled with distracting cares about the earth, what he shall eat and drink, and what he shall put on, how he shall provide for himself and his family, and what shall become of him. Though he is well now, what may become of him afterwards? When the heart is filled with distracting cares about the things of the earth, as far as the heart has these prevailing over it, so far such a man may be judged to be earthly.

There are but two things that cause distracting cares about any business. The first is an apprehension of some very great evil. In case I should be disappointed, I look upon my disappointment as a most intolerable evil to me. If I should be disappointed, I do not know what in the world to do. The second is an uncertainty in the means for the prevention of this disappointment. When I look upon disappointment as a great evil, I cannot trust those things that prevent and help me against disappointment to do so. I see them as being too weak to help me; notwithstanding such means, I may yet be disappointed. This causes distracting thoughts.

So, in the things of the earth, an earthly-minded man or woman has his or her thoughts filled with distracting cares about the world. First, looking upon the things of the world as such great things, they think that if they are disappointed they will be undone. They look upon it as such a fearful, insufferable evil to be deprived of their estate and outward comforts in this world. Second, they don't look upon the means of provision for themselves and their families as having any certainty in it, which is a main thing to be considered. As for outward things in the world, they find by experience that there is uncertainty in them. And then for any promise that there is in Scripture that God will provide for them and their families, alas, that they dare not trust. That's a thing that of all means they think to be the weakest. "Lord, have mercy upon us," they say. If they have nothing else to trust but a word of Scripture, they think of themselves as being most miserable and wretched.

But now, it would be otherwise with the soul if it were not earthly-minded. It would not be at any great pause how things fall out here in the matters of the world. It's true, perhaps I may miscarry in such a business; and my estate may be taken from me by the Chaldeans or the Sabeans, as was Job's; but I shall not be undone, my happiness is not gone. I shall have that which will comfort me when all that is gone. Suppose the worst, yes, this will not undo me.

Indeed, a man who sends his whole estate abroad in a venture is very solicitous because, if there is bad news about it, he is undone. But another man who has a great deal of riches, house, and lands, and a stock at home to maintain him and his family, if bad news comes he thinks, "I have a stock at home to live on." He is not as solicitous. So a worldly man has all his stock in the earth; there's his only portion, and if he miscarries there, he is undone. But a godly man, though he has the things of the earth, yet he has something else, treasures in heaven to rest upon besides the earth, and therefore he is not as solicitous.

And then, as for the uncertainty of means and help, if a godly man looks upon outward causes, he sees all is uncertain, but he has a promise to rest upon: "I will never leave you nor forsake you. Cast your care upon Me for I care for you." This he looks on as a certain means and help. Whatever falls out, here's a promise that he can build upon, and therefore this takes off his solicitous cares. But an earthly-minded man's heart is filled with distracting cares because he looks upon himself as undone if he miscarries here and has nothing more than the creature does for his provision in this world.

5. An earthly-minded man or woman is one whose great business of heart, and the endeavors of his life, are about the things of the earth. He makes it his great business; and the strong endeavors of his spirit are exercised in the things of the earth. He eagerly and greedily works with the strongest intention about these things; how the whole soul, the whole man is laid out about the world; it is the adequate object of his soul.

You will say, "Other men are busy in their callings as well as these whom you account earthly-minded men." Yes, but they are busy in their callings in obedience to God. And, for outward things, they set aside their obedience to God. Then all the things that they busy themselves with in the world, were it not under that consideration that they were obeying God in it, they would not be adequate objects for their souls. By an adequate object, I mean that which is sufficient to take up the whole strength of the soul to lay it out fully.

I'll give you this example to show you what I mean by an adequate object. You have a little child playing sports. This sport has as much in it as there is in his spirit; there is a kind of equality between his spirit and such a sport. A child receives enough benefit from a sport that it's worth laying out all his strength and might upon it. Now, it may be, sometimes a man or woman will play with their child. They will play as the child does, but this sport is not an adequate object. A man or woman will play with the child for awhile, but there is not enough good in this play to fill their souls, though it is fully adequate to the desires of the child. These things are not fully adequate to the desires of a man or woman. They have other matters in their heads than these, and businesses of a higher nature. And so it is in those who are not earthly-minded. Though they may be busied about the things of this world, yet they use the world as if they used it not. The things of the world are not adequate objects to their hearts. A spiritual heart reserves the chief strength of it for higher things. I follow these things in the world, but I reserve the chief strength for a more desirable good.

Suppose a man has friends come to him, and perhaps some of an ordinary rank come first. He makes ordinary provision for them; but if he has any choice things for entertaining, he reserves them for some choice friends who are coming. So a man who is not of the world, though he may be busy in earthly things, yet the choice of his heart he reserves for things of a higher nature. I remember Tertullian had a speech of the Christians, how they ate and drank when they supped. "They ate and drank so as they remembered they were to pray that night before they slept." So a gracious, spiritual heart follows his outward business in the world, but remembers that he is to converse with God that night before he sleeps, so that he reserves the strength of his spirit for communion with God. But the other lays out all his strength as if he had nothing to do afterwards. In this, an earthly and a spiritual heart are quite contrary.

The apostle would have godly men to use the world as if they used it not. Contrarily, an earthly-minded man uses spiritual things as if he used them not. How an earthly-minded man's heart is in spiritual things, so a spiritual mind is in earthly things. An earthly-minded man will do some things that are spiritual. He will come and hear the Word, perhaps he will pray in his family and read a chapter, but his heart is not there. He does it as if he did it not, come and hears as if he heard not,

and prays as if he prayed not. He does not make it his business
to pray or hear. A spiritually-minded man does worldly things
as if he did them not, in comparison to being busy in spiritual
things. Those he does with all his might. An earthly-minded
man is like Corah, Dathan, and Abiram. We read that they were
swallowed up by the earth. So, the truth is, the things of the
earth, contentments, provision for themselves and families in
earthly things, opens and swallows up the very hearts of earthly-
minded men.

6. Suppose a man does not seem to be so strongly inclined
to lay out his whole strength and heart about earthly things.
Yet when any man or woman shall seek any earthly thing for
itself, and not in subordination to some higher good, this is an
earthly-minded man, for as this prevails, in 2 Corinthians 4:18,
our Apostle Paul speaks of the things that are seen that are but
temporal. While we look not at the things that are seen, for the
things that are seen are earthly and temporal. The word is as
much as if to say, "While we look upon temporal and earthly
things that are seen, we do not make them our end. We seek
them in subordination. There is something else that we look at
as higher in all these things."

For instance, a man who is godly follows his business as
other men do, but what is it that he would have? It is this: I
show my obedience to God, and I would provide those things
that may be helpful to me to serve God in my generation; that's
my end. I can appeal to God in this, that even in following my
business and all outward things, it is so that I might follow God
in the use of means for the providing of such things as may
enable me to serve him the more in my generation. This is my
scope in what I do.

But now on the other side, an earthly-minded man makes
his scope to follow his business and look about the business of

his calling that he might gain. He would get that he might get; he would have more that he might have more, and that he and his children might be somebody in the world. It may be that he might have enough to have his will and lusts, and therefore he follows his business very intently, merely that he may get to satisfy the flesh. Yes, indeed, all the good things that he does, he brings them in subordination to earthly things. You may take it thusly, a spiritual man does not seek earthly things for himself, but an earthly man does. Or, more fully, an earthly man is earthly in all that he does do, both in earthly and spiritual things; and a spiritually-minded man is spiritual in all he does, both in spiritual and in earthly things. When an earthly man is in earthly things he is altogether earthly; he does not look at obedience to God in what he does. A spiritual man says, "I'll follow my calling because God has required it," but an earthly man thinks, "I'll follow it because I see gain coming from it." This is earthly. Though the things are lawful, (and it's your duty to follow your calling) but to follow it merely for gain, this is earthly. But because it is your duty and it is the place God has set you in, that is spirituality in earthly things. An earthly man is earthly in earthly things, and he is more earthly in spiritual things. When he performs spiritual duties, he has an earthly end in it, either to get esteem from men, or to cover some evil. Perhaps merely for form or fashion he does it in an earthly way, and it may be at most that he does it merely for his own quiet, to satisfy his own conscience.

Now a spiritual man is spiritual in earthly things. One of a spiritual mind is more heavenly and spiritual when he is about his calling, though it be the lowest, like cutting hedges, digging ditches, pulling ropes or lines, or using his axe or hammer. He is more spiritual at these than is an earthly man when he is praying or hearing, or receiving Sacraments. Certainly it is so, and it will be found to be so at the great day of judgment, when all the secrets of all hearts shall be disclosed.

7. An earthly-minded person is earthly in spiritual things. I grant that the best of the saints may have some earthliness in spiritual things, but I speak of the predominance. It's that which rules in the heart, so that in the performance of spiritual things, his very ends are but earthly, and the frame of his heart is but earthly in spiritual performances.

8. An earthly-minded man passes through many and great difficulties in matters of the earth, and they are very little to him. Though he toils a great deal in matters of the earth he is never weary because he is in his proper element. Therefore, let there be what difficulties there will be, which to another man would be very great, he makes them as nothing and, though there is much toil and labor, yet he is not weary. Why? Because he is in his own element. The fish is not weary with swimming, but a man is quickly weary. It is because the fish is in his element and the man is not. Observe this, when a man's spirit is in this kind of temper, let him be busied about earthly things, wherein earthly advantage comes in, no difficulties will hinder him, no wind or weather. He will rise in cold mornings and go abroad, do anything in the world. Oh! What difficulties will men endure in storms at sea, and hazards there and troubles at land, and sit up late, and rise early, and toil themselves, and complain of no weariness or difficulties. But, let them come to spiritual things, to soul business that concerns God and their spiritual estates. Every little difficulty puts them aside and discourages them. Every molehill is a mountain in their way. I would do so and so, but it's so hard, and 'tis tedious to rise in a morning, especially in cold winters. It is very hard and difficult to read and pray. And so he complains of the difficulty of these things.

To watch over the heart is a very difficult thing. To an

earthly man, any spiritual thing is difficult and the difficulties discourage him. In spiritual things, oh, how weary are they! In Malachi 1:13, they cry out, "What a weariness is it!" But they can follow the business of the world from morning to night and never get tired. They can work like a horse and never be out of breath! I wish you would try once to spend one Sabbath exactly and see what a weariness that would be to you. Resolve just one Sabbath to rise early in the morning, and to have your thoughts spiritual and heavenly as much as you can. Then get up and pray alone in your closet. Then read, hear, and meditate, and mark what you hear. And when you go home, think of it and confer about it. And when you come again to attend on the Word, and so spend the whole day in hearing, reading, meditating, and conferencing about good things, calling your family to account, and praying again. See how tiresome this will be to your hearts if they are carnal.

However, a spiritual heart will call the Sabbath a delight. And the Sabbath unto such a one is no other than a type and forerunner of that eternal day of rest it shall enjoy in the kingdom of heaven. One who is spiritual counts the Sabbath to be a day of rest, but an earthly man is quickly tired in spiritual things. He will give up his work and not go through it. We read in Nehemiah 4:6 that Nehemiah spoke of the great difficulties that they met with in their work, and yet the work went on, for they had a mind to it. So look how a man's mind is; he will be able to go through with his work. If a man is an earthly-minded man, he will go through with his work. If he takes up worldly business, he will go through with it for he has a mind to it. He is an earthly-minded man. But let him take on a spiritual work and he will lay it aside before it is half done! He will seldom bring to perfection any spiritual work. Why? Because he has no mind to it, whereas, if the heart were spiritual and there were any spiritual work undertaken, such a one would go through with it until all was finished.

9. An earthly-minded man is one who conceives the most heavenly truths that are revealed in the Word in an earthly way, according to his mind, his genius, and the disposition of his own heart. I truly think this is meant in a special manner in this place, for the apostle is speaking of those who opposed him in his ministry and who were enemies to the cross of Christ. Now, these mind earthly things; their minds are of an earthly temper, and therefore it is no wonder they do not savor those heavenly and spiritual truths that we bring to them for their minds, being earthly, only apprehend those things after an earthly manner.

Now what was the great truth that the apostle brought to the Philippians? It was the way of reconciling the world to God, of making our peace with God, and of our justification through Jesus Christ. Now there is no point of religion that is more spiritual, heavenly, and divine than the doctrine of reconciliation, and of justification by Jesus Christ. So that one who is of an earthly disposition, though he may be convinced of a necessity of pardon of sin and peace with God, yet apprehends the making of his peace with God and obtaining pardon of sin in an earthly manner. He has carnal thoughts and apprehensions about his place with God and obtaining pardon of sin. He thinks it is the same way that one man obtains peace with another when there has been a falling out, and of getting pardon from another man whom he has offended. He conceives it in an earthly way; he looks upon his making peace with God by some thing that he must perform. But the free justification by the grace of God in Christ? It's too divine, spiritual, and heavenly for an earthly-minded man to apprehend. An earthly-minded man's apprehensions of God are only in a carnal, earthly way.

As the prophet speaks in Isaiah 1:3, "The ox knows his owner, and the ass his master's crib," in the same way an earthly-minded man knows God like an ox knows his owner, and the ass his master. The ox knows his owner since he brings him fodder daily; so an earthly-minded man has no other apprehensions of God but that God gives him good things in this world. God makes his corn to grow or prospers his voyage. An earthly-minded man may rise so high as to have apprehensions of God as bringing good things unto him here on earth, but one who is spiritual and heavenly apprehends God as God. He does not look upon God merely as good in respect of the benefit he receives from God here, but he looks upon God as He is in Himself. He sees the face of God. There's a great deal of difference between a man who knows another man and a beast that knows a man.

The ox knows his owner. The ox knows the man who brings hay or provisions to him, but a man knows a man in another way. He knows what the nature of a man is, what it is to be a rational creature. So one who is spiritual knows what God is in Himself; he sees the face of God, and understands what God is in another way than others do. The difference between the knowledge of God that a spiritual soul has, one who is pure in heart, and the knowledge of God that an earthly heart has, is just as different. As the ox knows the man who drives him to fat pastures, so an earthly man knows God gives him good things. But a spiritual man knows God as one man knows another, not in the full excellency, but there is such a difference in some degree between the apprehensions of God in a spiritual heart and the apprehensions of God in an earthly heart.

We might mention many other spiritual and divine truths that an earthly mind apprehends only in an earthly way. For example, consider heaven itself. How does an earthly mind apprehend that? He apprehends that he shall be delivered from pain and shall have some kind of glory, but he knows not what it is. He conceives it according to the way of the earth, some pompous, glorious thing, that he shall live in pleasures and not in pain, and so apprehends all the glory of heaven but in sensuality. A spiritual heart looks at heaven in another way. He looks upon the enjoyment of communion with God and Jesus Christ in heaven, and living the life of God in heaven. That's a thing an earthly heart has no skill in at all, neither does such a heart so much as savor it.

Thus I have in these several particulars revealed what an earthly-minded man is. Oh, that you would lay your hands upon your hearts and consider how far these things reach you! But besides these, I have divers other arguments to convince the consciences of men and women that there is still much earthliness in them, but we shall treat them in order later.

The second heading to consider is this: the great evil of earthly-mindedness is that they mind earthly things. "Is that such a great matter?" you say. "We cannot imagine the transcendency of the evil there is in this. We think there's a great deal of evil in swearing, whoring, drinking, and such scandalous sins. But to have an earthly mind? We do not think this to be such an exceeding evil." Yet you will find that the Scripture speaks most dreadful things against this, and if God is pleased to set them upon your hearts, I hope that much glory may come to God by it, and much good to you in particular.

CHAPTER THREE

Six Evils of Earthly-Mindedness

THE FIRST EVIL. The Scripture calls it adultery. It is spiritual adultery in James 4:4: "Ye adulterers and adulteresses, know ye not that the friendship of the world is enmity with God?" They were adulterers and adulteresses in respect of their love for the world. You who would abhor the thought of a temptation to adultery yet may commit spiritual adultery. A man or a woman may be an adulterer or adulteress before the Lord, though they never commit the act of uncleanness with another. Yet if their hearts are towards another, they are guilty of uncleanness; for Christ said that whoever looks on a woman to lust after her in his heart has committed adultery already. That is, he has sinned against that command which forbids adultery. If a man lets his heart go after another woman more than his wife, and a wife after another man more than her husband, this is adultery before the Lord. So if our hearts go after anything more than the Lord Jesus Christ, to whom we profess to be married and who is our Husband, this is adultery in Scriptural terms.

THE SECOND EVIL. A worldly or an earthly mind in Scriptural terms is called "idolatry" in Ephesians 5:5. Speaking of divers sins that should not so much as be named among them as is becoming saints, he lists covetousness among the rest. And he adds this, "and covetousness, which is idolatry." Now what is earthly-mindedness but covetousness, which is idolatry? A man or woman is an idolater who is of an earthly mind. Idolatry, which is worshipping sticks and stones, you all account to be a great sin; but do you and all others take heed of another idolatry that may be as bad, which is to have your hearts make the god of this world—the cursed mammon of unrighteousness—to be your God, to make the things of the earth to be your Christ by falling down and worshipping the golden calf of the world? It's certain that the thing a man's heart is most taken with and set upon is his god. And therefore, in this verse, it is said they made earthly things (their bellies) their god. The voluptuous and drunkards make their bellies their god, and the unclean person makes his strumpet to be his goddess and worships that.

Whatever your heart is most set upon, that is your god. Therefore, you must know that this is the meaning of the commandment, "Thou shalt have no other Gods before Me." That is, "You shall give Me, and nothing else, the strength of your soul. I am a God to My creature when I have its strength exercised about Me, to lift up Me as the highest good." But if there is anything else that your soul is set on as the highest good, that's your god, and it's worse than bowing the knee. You bow your soul to that thing.

Now the more base anything is that we make a god of, the more vile is the idolatry. When the Egyptians worshiped divers sorts of gods, they were accounted the most vile idolaters; whereas other heathens worshiped more excellent things—the sun, moon, and stars. The Egyptians worshiped dogs, cats, onions, and vile things, and therefore their idolatry was vile. So the more vile anything is that men or women set their hearts upon, the more vile is their idolatry. For a man to set his heart upon unclean lusts and to make them to be a god, satisfying those lusts, is abominable. To make any earthly thing a god to us is most vile for, of all the things of the works of creation that God has made, the earth is the lowest. It is the basest and lowest thing, and has the least beauty in itself; and it is the most dull and meanest element of all. To make earthly things to be a god to you is most vile.

OBJECTION: You will say for this idolatry, "What is there in it?" ANSWER: There are two particulars to open the evil of idolatry or earthly-mindedness:

First, the evil of idolatry is in this: you depart from God. In letting your hearts go out to these things, you go off from God and renounce the protection of God, the goodness and mercy of God. You leave it all by this. In Hosea 4:12, they are said to "go a-whoring from under their God." It is a notable phrase. By going to idols, they went out from the protection of God whereas, while they were worshipping the true God, they were under the protection of God. But when they went to idols, they went from under their God, from under His protection. So when you set your heart upon God and lift up the infinite First Being of all things as the Chief Good to your soul, you are under the influence of this grace and mercy; but when you depart from Him and make other things to be your chief good, you go from under His protection and from His goodness and mercy.

Second, God is slighted and condemned when you choose to make the earth your god rather than the infinite First Being of all things. A man might despise his wife, an abominable sin, and choose to go to a queen, the most beautiful woman in the world, forsaking his wife. But to leave a queen or an empress, who is the most beautiful woman upon earth, and to have the heart cleave to a base dunghill-raker, would this not be a great show of contempt to the beautiful queen? Yet it is so when you forsake the blessed, eternal God as your Chief Good, and choose the things of the earth. For the truth is that the earth is the sink of all the creatures of God's making; and for you to leave the most blessed and eternal One, and to make the earth your god, is, of necessity, a very vile and abominable thing. Therefore the prophet Jeremiah, in speaking of this idolatry, calls the heavens and the earth to be amazed at it. Jeremiah 2:12–13: "Be astonished, O ye heavens at this, and be horrible afraid; be ye very desolate, saith the Lord." Why? What's the matter? "For My people have committed two evils: they have forsaken Me, the Fountain of living waters, and hewed them out cisterns, broken cisterns that can hold no water." So it is here. You forsake the Fountain of living waters, the blessed God, and your heart cleaves to the dust. You seek your contentment and happiness in cisterns that can hold no water! Let the heavens be astonished at this horrible wickedness.

THE THIRD EVIL. Earthly-mindedness is enmity against God. You would hate to be found an enemy against God. Certainly it's true that an earthly-minded man or woman is an enemy to God. The Scripture makes it to be enmity in James 4:4: "Know ye not that the love of the world is enmity to God?" Observe this, for there's much in it: if God would be pleased to lay this on our hearts, you will find by experience that earthly-mindedness makes men to be enemies to that which is spiritually good. Therefore, well might the Holy Ghost say 'tis enmity to God; for whatever is enmity to anything that is spiritually good is enmity to God. As much as my heart or any of your hearts are against anything that is spiritual, so much my heart, or any of your hearts, are enemies to God. Here in this text, the earthly-minded men are made enemies to the cross of Christ, that is, enemies to the spiritual preaching of Christ and holding forth of Christ. Indeed, if they would have mixed Christ and circumcision together, then they would have been content with it; but now this spiritual way of preaching Christ and being justified by faith alone, and Christian religion in its purity, was that which was not suitable to their carnal hearts, and therefore they were enemies to it.

Oh! Earthly-mindedness makes us enemies to spiritual things. Where you have greater enemies unto the things of God, unto spiritual things, unto the ministry of the Word and to the work of God's grace upon the hearts of men and women, there are no greater enemies unto these things than earthly-minded men, men who savor the things of the earth. They can go up and down, and they do not care as long as they can go about their business, grow rich in the world, and fare deliciously every day with Dives, making provision for the flesh to fulfill the lusts thereof. There is an antipathy in their spirits against Jesus Christ and all goodness.

THE FOURTH EVIL. There is scarcely any disposition more opposite, more contrary to the work of grace, to the work of godliness in a man's own heart, than earthly-mindedness. 'Tis so exceedingly cross to the nature of grace that you may as well put men or women on the stand, and put them upon examination whether there is any grace or not in their hearts, if earthly-mindedness prevails. If God should suffer your corruptions to prevail over you, so that you should break forth into some notorious sins, then it may be you would begin to think, "Can this stand with grace? And how can that stand with such workings as I have had before? Have I not cause to fear that I am but a hypocrite, a rotten professor?" This earthly-mindedness has as much opposition to the nature of grace and the power of godliness in the heart as almost any sin that you can name. It is quite contrary to the very beginning of the work of grace—not contrary to the degrees only, but to the very beginning! The main work of God, at first, in working grace in the soul is to disengage the soul from the creature. It is to take it off from the earth, and from all creatures here below. It is naturally true that as we are of the earth, so we are earthly and have our spirits engaged to the things of the earth. But then comes the work of grace upon the soul and takes it off, and discharges the heart from the earth. Therefore you find that Christ lays this in as the first lesson, "He that will be My disciple must deny himself, and take up his cross and follow Me." It is as if He should say, "Never think of being a Christian unless you will deny yourselves." Self? What's that? It is all natural contentment, natural self, and sinful self.

To be emptied wholly of yourselves, and creature comforts, and contentments, and take up His cross, to be willing to suffer anything in regard to earthly comforts, to be willing to lay down all at His feet, to give up your interest in all, and to take up His cross, this is the very first beginning of Christ's bringing disciples to Himself. The soul then says, "Let me have my sin pardoned, and farewell earth; it's heaven, holiness, renewal in the image of God, communion and union with God, and living to the eternal praise of His name in Christ that my heart is upon." This is in the beginning of God's working the heart to Himself.

The work of grace, when it is first wrought, has the name of "vocation" or "calling." What is it for a man to be called? "Give diligence to make your calling and election sure." To be called is this: whereas before you were altogether digging and delving in the earth and seeking for your happiness in the world, it pleased God to make you hear a voice behind you, calling you and telling you, "O poor soul, your happiness is not here. There are other things in which the Chief Good consists. You were made for higher and better things than these. God has nobler thoughts about mankind than merely to let him have a few contentments here in the earth. Oh soul! Come away and look after higher things."

Here's the first work of grace. And the soul answers unto this call of God and says, "Lord, I come," and so the soul goes up to God to dispose of earthly things; and this is the beginning of the work of grace. Now how contrary is earthly-mindedness to the work of God in bringing grace into the heart? Think of it in these three things.

1. The very work of conversion is set out in Scripture by God's calling the soul out of the world: "Whom He hath predestinated, him He hath called." When God effectually begins to work upon the heart of a sinner, He causes a voice to be heard in the soul. "O soul! You have been busying yourself about many things, but there is one thing necessary. Oh, come out of that way of yours that you are in. You can never be happy otherwise. You will be undone in it." The Lord calls the soul out of the world, and that is the very work of conversion, the soul's answering to God's call. Now, can the soul answer God's call and still have a heart cleaving to these things? Surely such a one is not yet effectually called out of the world.

2. From this follows the soul's answer to this call. The Lord disengages the heart from all creature comforts, and teaches the first lesson: to deny himself and take up Christ's cross. Now, what is more opposite to self-denial and taking up the cross of Christ than earthly-mindedness? The text here says, "They are enemies to the cross of Christ."

3. A third thing in conversion is the resigning up of the soul to God as the Chief Good. The soul, upon the call of God, learns the lesson of self-denial and taking up the cross; and so being disengaged from the creature, now resigns itself to God as an infinite, soul-satisfying good forever. Now you cannot but in the naming of this see how opposite earthly-mindedness is to it.

Next we turn to the work of grace upon the heart, after the heart is converted and turned to God.

First, grace brings a new light into the soul. A spiritual and divine light is set up in the soul upon the conversion of a sinner to God. But the earth, you know, is the dark part of the world; and earthly-mindedness causes darkness to be upon the spirit, as the interposition of the earth between us and the sun hinders the sight of the sun from us. So the interposition that there is of earthliness in the soul of man between God and itself hinders the sight of God from the soul. There is a divine light set up in the soul, and God works grace that discovers things of a higher and more excellent and glorious nature than those things were which before the soul so greatly cleaved to.

In the second place, the Scripture sets forth the work of grace by the phrase, "the new creature." In the soul, all things are made new and old things are passed away. He who is in Christ is a new creature. Now, earthly-mindedness is opposite to the new creation of the soul. It's the old man who is of the earth. The first man is of the earth, earthly; and so it is apparent that you are still only in the stock of the first man, of the earth, who is an earthly-minded man. But the second man is the Lord from heaven. But now you who are an earthly-minded man or woman are yet but a child of Adam, the first man, and so are of the earth, earthly. This is opposed to grace, for grace works a new creation in the soul.

Third, grace is of an elevating nature. It raises the heart above itself and above the creature, yea, above the world, in some respect above angels themselves, above principalities and powers, above all created things. Grace is of a raising nature, but an earthly-minded man sinks down to low and base things.

Fourth, grace is of an enlarging nature. It enlarges the heart so that it cannot be satisfied with any earthly thing. Though God should give the whole world to a heart that has grace, this would not satisfy that heart. Why? Because it is so enlarged by the work of grace. The work of grace is the divine nature, the image of God in the soul, and therefore makes the soul like God. It's said of God in Isaiah 40:15 that all the nations of the earth are to Him but as a drop in the bucket, and as the final dust in the balance. Now, grace makes the soul to be like God, to account all the things of the earth to be as a drop in the bucket, and the dust of the balance, to be nothing, less than nothing.

Fifth, grace sanctifies the soul. Now, what is it to sanctify but to take off from all common uses, and to dedicate to God as the highest act of all things? Therefore, the Greek word for "holy" is a word that signifies the earth, as if to say, "not earthly." And the phrase "a holy one" in the Greek language is literally "not an earthly one," according to the usual etymology given to it. Now, grace makes the soul holy. It sanctifies the soul. It sets apart the soul for God, and dedicates and consecrates the soul to God. And therefore you see that earthly-mindedness is opposed to the work of God in bringing grace into the soul, and to the work of grace, and the power of godliness in the soul of man. This is the great evil of earthly-mindedness.

THE FIFTH EVIL. Earthly-mindedness puts men upon very great temptations. For that we need no other Scripture than

1 Timothy 6:9, where the apostle says, "But they that will be rich fall into a temptation and a snare." Mark it, those who have set their hearts so much upon the things of the earth are resolved that they must have whatever comes from it. Note the phrase, they who will be rich apprehend a necessity of the things of the earth. They do not only wish and desire, "Oh, that we had riches and these things of the earth," but they resolve that they must have them upon any terms.

If the heart goes on in obedience to God in the duties of its calling, and if God sends in riches and an estate, it thankfully accepts it from God. These do not meet with such temptations and a snare as the apostle speaks of here. But when the heart is set upon it, that it must have an estate no matter what, they who will be so fall into temptations and a snare. There are dangerous temptations in following after the things of the earth, and there is a snare in them that you do not think of. You think only of the splendor of the things of the earth, how sumptuously you should live and how fine you should be, in your house, in your clothes, and what table you may keep. You only think of those things that may give the flesh contentment. But you do not think of the temptation and the snare that is in them; and those whose hearts are set upon these thing fall into the snare, the temptation.

Those who are earthly-minded have great temptations, to shift up and down, to strain their consciences for the things of the earth. For so it is that while we live in this world, God has made the things of the earth to be as thorns, and so they are compared in Scripture. It's hard for one to meddle with thorns without pricking his fingers. They are as briars, and it's hard for the sheep to get among them without losing some of her wool. In the same way, it's hard for the heart to be busy about the things of the earth without it being pricked and losing some of its fleece. It will fall into temptation and a snare and be caught. Oh, how many men and women have enlightened consciences, and think sometimes that they would not do anything against their consciences for all the world, though they might gain all the glory and riches under heaven! But with earthly hearts, when it comes to some particular, how ready are they! At least to strain conscience and not to attend to the voice of conscience, and they are willing that conscience should have its mouth stopped for the time being. Indeed, if their consciences plainly told them that this thing is absolutely a sin against God, perhaps they would not do it. But that is not the snare, for it is no snare when I see the danger before me. Here's a deep pit, and if I step one step further I will fall into it. This is no snare.

There are few who will be caught by a pit that's open; so the devil will lay some green grass upon the pit so that they will not perceive the danger. Such as have earthly hearts fall into a snare and temptation. They are put upon straining their conscience and wringing it as much as may be, and they are put to many shifts. Oh! Once a man is in an earthly business, he does not know how in the world to bear it if he gets crossed in it. "It may be I have gone thus far, and I have great hopes that I shall succeed in it, only there is one stop." Now, for him to think that this one stop may cost him all, how it goes to his heart. But now, if you will strain your conscience a little, you may get over it presently. An earthly man will strain hard but he will get over it; but were a man's heart taken off from the earth, though he had never gone so far in business, if there should come a stop in a matter of conscience, just a doubt that such a thing was a sin would be enough to stop him. A mere doubt lest he should sin would be enough to make him say, "Let the business fall if it will, there may be a snare in this, and I see some cause to doubt." Now, if the heart were spiritual, it would be taken off;

but an earthly mind will go through many dreadful things, and does not trouble itself, and so ensnares itself exceedingly that it may get an estate, or preserve it once he has it.

THE SIXTH EVIL. The sixth thing wherein the danger of earthly-mindedness consists is this: 'tis one of the greatest hindrances in the world to profiting from the ministry of the Word. Oh, many of you cannot but be convinced in your consciences that you have not profited by the Word; and sometimes you will complain of the lack of profiting under the means! Oh, that you had hearts to look into the cause of it, as to why it is that you profit so little! It will appear that it comes from your earthly-mindedness. You bring a heart full of the world, full of dross, with you. It is no wonder that you do not see those spiritual, heavenly things that are in the Word when there is so much dross in your eyes.

Summer travelers, traveling in the midst of dust and in company, do not have the freedom of their eyes to see things like they do at other times. Oh, many men come to the Word with their thick clay, and a great deal of filth that clams up their very eyes, and deadens their hearts in the hearing of the Word! You know what Christ said to Martha, when Mary was sitting at Christ's feet and hearing His Word. He said that Martha was encumbered with many things. So it is many times with those who come to hear the Word. Though they are in the presence of Christ and have the sound of the Word in their ears, yet their hearts are encumbered about many things. There's a great noise in their hearts. They are busied in the world even while they are hearing the Word. As you find in Ezekiel 33:31, there's a notable description which, I fear, may be true of many of you: "And they come unto thee as the people cometh, and they sit before thee as My people, and they hear thy words, but they will not do them; for with their mouth they show much love, but their heart goeth after their covetousness."

Notice, "They sit before you as My people, and they hear your words, and they show much love with their mouth." They will commend the sermon. It may be that they will say, "He is an excellent preacher; it was a very good sermon that we heard today." They will show love with their mouths, but yet their hearts go after their covetousness for all that. They heard a man speak fine things, and bring excellent expressions to set forth the matter at hand, but their hearts are after the things of the earth, and after their covetousness.

They had carnal, earthly, drossy hearts, and hence it was that no good came to them by the ministry of the Word. That famous place, which shows it clearly, is in Matthew 13:22. You know the several sorts of ground that had the seed of the Word sown into them, but there was but one of them that was good and faithful. The other was thorny ground. He who received seed among the thorns is he that hears the Word; and the cares of this world and the deceitfulness of riches chokes the Word and it becomes unfruitful. I beseech you to observe it: these of whom our Savior speaks of herein this parable, who get no benefit from the Word, are not men who live lewdly (drunkards, swearers, or whore-masters), but those who have earthly hearts. It says, "the deceitfulness of riches." The things of the earth do not hinder in an open way, for thousands of men who have earthly hearts do not know that they have earthly hearts. No, it is the deceitfulness of riches, and it chokes the Word. It may be, just when they are hearing the Word, if affects them. Oh, they think it's sweet, and they will remember it; but the deceitfulness of riches and the cares of this world choke the Word. When these things come, they have worldly businesses, and their houses, and gardens, and comings in, and full tables, and all the delights that they have in the world—all these things come and possess the heart so that the Word is choked. It cannot get down into the soul to sink in there, and so to prevail in the soul to bring forth fruit. The Word is choked.

Many of you come here three times on the Lord's Day, and have precious seed sown all those times; and yet how it is choked by the cares of this world and the deceitfulness of the things of this world! You bring with you, and keep with you, and carry along with you, earthly minds; and hence it is that the Word does not prevail with your hearts. Oh! What do you lose through this earthliness? You lose the fruit of the Word that should save your souls. A spiritual heart, having received some one truth into it, later blesses God for it, and would not for ten thousand worlds have it otherwise than that he should have that truth preached unto his heart at such a time. Oh, he has cause to bless God for such a morning, for such a day, that he has such a godly pearl of great price presented to him! Taking root, it's more than if God had given him thousands of worlds to possess.

But now many of you, having your thoughts and hearts about some petty thing of this world, all those blessed truths that you hear from time to time, things that the very angels desire to pry into, are all choked and come to be unfruitful. Why did the young man who came to Christ to know what he should do to inherit eternal life receive no good? The text says that he had great possessions. A man may, no doubt, be a rich man and yet a godly man, a holy man. But it was the heart, mixed with the earth, that hindered the young man from embracing Jesus Christ.

Young men are, for the most part, guilty of fleshliness rather than seeking after the riches of the world. Yet sometimes it has been the bane of some young men. They were very forward when they were servants; oh, how precious was the Word to them! But when they got into the world and found the sweetness of it coming in, then the Word was choked in them, and they have lost the savor they had in the Word. They have lost the relish of the Word. It is not as sweet now to them as formerly it had been.

That's the great evil of earthly-mindedness: it hinders the great benefit of the Word, and there is much evil in this. If you had hearts to receive what is delivered, your hearts would tremble at the thought of this. "O Lord! What shall I do so as not to be hindered in profiting from this Word?" 'Tis the great blessing of God to the world. It's that which must save my soul; there's more worth in it than ten thousand worlds. Whatsoever might hinder my profiting from Thy Word, I must take heed of it. Take heed of earthly-mindedness. Many of your consciences cannot but tell you this. Sometimes any business will keep an earthly-minded man from coming to the Word; and when he does come, there is earth in his heart and ears that keeps him from attending upon the Word. When your thoughts are about earthly things in the hearing of a sermon, it may be that some truth passes by your soul that might have saved you eternally, and you have lost that opportunity which, perhaps, you shall never have again.

CHAPTER FOUR

Eight Additional Evils of Earthly-Mindedness

THE SEVENTH EVIL. Earthly-mindedness causes many foolish lusts in the heart, and that's a great evil. I will expand them in six particulars. You have the same Scripture as was used previously for the temptations and snare, 1 Timothy 6:9: "But they that will be rich fall into a temptation and a snare, and into many foolish and hurtful lusts," lusts that are very foolish and simple.

Particular 1. It causes men to follow after things that are very vile and mean. It causes men to bestow the strength of their immortal souls on things that have no worth at all in them. That's a foolish lust, to bestow the strength of an immortal soul on vanities. If you should see men of excellent gifts spending their time on trifles and toys, like catching flies or chasing feathers, you would say that they had begun to be dull-minded. So the soul of man, capable of such excellency as it is—of communion with God, with the Father, Son, and Holy Ghost—to have its strength spent on such poor, trifling things that cannot profit in the evil day, oh, this is a foolish lust!

Particular 2. Foolish lusts, or earthly-mindedness, cause you to be a servant to your servants. You would think a man is a fool who is a servant to his servants. God has made the things of the earth to be servants to you, and yet you come and place your neck under your servant's yoke and become a servant to your servant! Yea, is it not a great folly for a man to expect all his honors and respect to come from a servant rather than from any excellence in himself?

Suppose a man is traveling and is shown some respect, but for his servant's sake rather than for his own. Once he realized this, he would account it a great dishonor to himself. But an earthly heart puts itself into such a condition, since it is its greatest honor to have honors from its estate and riches. Earthly men do not respect other men for any worth that is in them, or for any excellency of their own, but for their riches alone, which is to say that a man is not respected for himself, but for his servant!

Take some men who have had estates, but are now deprived of them and have become as poor as almsmen or beggars. Who regards them now? But, let a man have grace and holiness, if he loses all and is made as poor as Job, yet he is one whom the angels of heaven look upon with honor, and would glory in attending. This is the difference between the carnal, earthly heart and the spiritual heart. It's a foolish lust to make yourself to be a servant to your servants.

Particular 3. Earthly-mindedness brings a man into foolish lusts, for a man might have much more of the earth if he did not mind it as much as he does. For a man to mind the earth and to endanger himself in doing so, when he might have it better not to do so, is surely a foolish thing. For a man to bestow a great deal of labor on a thing, when he might have it with less labor, is surely foolish. If you are one who belongs to God, you may expect God to bless you if you keep your hearts more spiritual. You might expect that God would grant you more of the good things of this world if you were less earthly-minded than you are. And it's your earthly-mindedness that makes God cut you short of these things. I am persuaded that there are many who have had bad success in their earthly affairs, and it's a fruit of God's displeasure upon them because their hearts are so much on worldly business. Were you to go on in your employment in obedience to God and commit it to God for success, you might be crowned with more success than you have been. Now what a foolish thing is this?

Particular 4. Yea, further, it's a great folly for any of you to buy a thing and pay a greater price for it than it is worth. Suppose you sent a servant to buy something, and when he returned you asked him what it cost, and he told you that he paid ten times more than it is worth. You would think you had sent a fool to the market. So an earthly-minded man manifests himself to God, His angels, and all the saints to be a fool. How? You bestow upon this world that which is a thousand times more worthy than the things of this world. You bestow upon this world that which might bring you to heaven.

I may say to an earthly-minded man, "Those thoughts, cares, affections, and endeavors that you spend on the things of the world, had they been spent on the things of God, they might have saved your soul to all eternity! You might have gotten Christ, heaven, and eternity. The Lord would have gone along with you, and you may come to say at the great day when all things shall be opened before men and angels, 'Had I spent those thoughts and cares and endeavors on understanding the ways and things of God and eternal life, my soul might have been saved forever!' " Not that our works will do it, but that God would have gone along together with you in those ways.

Now for you to spend those thoughts and cares on that

which you may never have (for many men and women spend their souls on things of the world and never have them), this is a sad thing. Oh! Will this not be a folly? Will you not curse yourself hereafter for your folly? "Oh, that I should spend myself and be spent on that which I have not gotten, and I must be damned for that. Whereas, had I spent time on things that concerned my soul and eternal life, I would have been more likely to have gotten those things."

God does not fail men in spiritual things as He does in earthly things. A man may be as diligent as is possible in earthly business and yet miscarry. But show me a man or woman who was ever diligent in seeking the things of God and eternal life and miscarried! I truly believe that, at the day of judgment, there will not be found one man who shall be able to say, "Lord, I improved the talents that Thou gavest me to the uttermost to save my soul, but, Lord, I was not able to do any more without Thy grace. Thou denied Thy grace to me and, therefore, now I must be damned."

I believe there will not be any soul who will be able to say this. But in the matters of the world, men do say that they have done all they could, labored and toiled, and yet for all this they miscarry. Oh, what a foolish thing is this, then, to toil and labor on that which is so uncertain; for is it not a foolish thing for a man to bestow all his estate on buying stones, on that which will not afford him any benefit at all? This folly is in the heart of man.

Two of you might go to the Indies, where there are precious stones. And one might purchase a cargo of precious stones and other rich commodities, while the other, with an equal amount of money, lays out all his money on baubles and trifles. Both went out with the same amount, both came home loaded, but one came home with precious stones that made him and his posterity great while the other brought home nothing but stones that made his neighbors scorn and jeer him. Oh, how would he tear his flesh for his folly in this matter!

This will be the difference between men and women at the day of judgment for, the truth is, what is this world but a seafare? We are sailing in this world, with either a load of pearls, or with that which has no worth at all. When you live in the times of the gospel, there is a market for pearls, for those things that will enrich you to all eternity. One man bestows all the strength of his thoughts and heart on those things for which he shall be blessing God in the highest heavens to all eternity, and the other bestows his thoughts and heart on the things of the earth, loading himself down with thick clay. There is a man or woman who shall be blessed for all of eternity, who shall join with angels and saints in the highest heavens to magnify the free grace of God in Christ. And there is another who, had he bestowed his thoughts and heart on the same things, might have been blessed forever also; but he, minding the things of the earth, is a cursed fool and is the scorn and contempt of men and angels to all eternity.

Earthly-mindedness brings men into foolish lusts. Oh! Men of earthly minds think themselves the only blessed men, and applaud themselves at home. Let men think what they will, the Holy Ghost said that those lusts caused by earthly-mindedness are foolish lusts.

Particular 5. It is folly for a man to do that which he must undo to gain. This is especially true of those earthly-minded men who have this earthliness so prevailing upon them as to get some earthly thing by some false ways. Such men must undo all they have done. You have gotten so much of the earth in some cunning, cheating way, and you bless yourselves that you found out such a mystery of iniquity. This is a foolish lust. Foolish?

Why? Because it must be done again. Either you must eternally be damned, or else you must restore as Zaccheus did, if you are able, even though it might make you impoverished. All the sorrow and repentance that can be will not be sufficient. You cannot be pardoned, even with all your sorrow and repentance, if you do not restore, if you are able, what you have gotten by ill means.

I do not know that there was ever any minister of the gospel on the face of the earth who did not hold to this, that it was of absolute necessity to salvation to restore. And this one reason cannot but satisfy any man's conscience, that a man cannot truly repent of a sin and yet willfully continue in it! Unless you restore, you are willfully continuing in that sin. Why? You do not only wrong the man the first hour, but as long as you keep anything that is his, you wrong him still. If you are able to restore and do not, simply because you are loath to part with so much money or so many goods, you willfully continue in the sin. Now, no man or woman can truly repent of a sin and yet willfully persist in that sin. What a foolish lust is this, for a man or woman to get the things of this world in such a way that he must undo it all, though it is to his shame.

Oh, consider what a folly it is! You deceitful servants who spend away on your lusts that which you cheat your master of. Afterwards, when you come to set yourself up, you must restore what you have stolen; and it may be that a great part of your estate must be repaid by way of restitution. It must be done, there's no way around it. Therefore, what a foolish lust it is to be so set upon the things of this earth as to get them in an earthly way.

Particular 6. By earthly-mindedness, they lose the comfort of earthly things before they have them. For example, suppose a man or woman has troubling thoughts about the things of the earth. It may be that, by their inordinate thoughts, cares, and affections about some earthly things, they contract much guilt. Yet after this, perhaps, God gives them that earthly thing. Now when they have it, if they have any light in their consciences, their convicted consciences will then reflect thusly: "I have this indeed, but do I have it with the blessing of God? I have it in my custody, but I got it dearly; it cost me such thoughts and cares and affections. Now I have it, but I cannot say it comes out of God's love. I rather fear that God has given it to me in His wrath because I got it in such a way."

Now all the comfort is gone and lost, whereas, had it come in the way of God, and had you given up yourself to God and let Providence bring such a comfort to you, you might have enjoyed much of God in it and blessed God for it. "The Lord has blessed me in my trading. Oh, I have it from the love of God." But now, because your heart was earthly before it came, when it does come you have no comfort in it. The comfort of all is lost before it comes, you have spent so much upon it. As when a man gets something, and after he gets it he thinks thusly, "What has this cost me? It has cost me a great deal more than it's worth; now the comfort of it has vanished."

THE EIGHTH EVIL. Earthly-mindedness is the root of apostasy. I'll give you but one Scripture and compare it with another. 2 Timothy 4:10 is a notable text that shows how earthly-mindedness breeds apostasy. 'Tis the example of Demas. The apostle said, "Demas hath forsaken me." What was the matter? "Having loved this present world." It was that which made Demas to be an apostate. Why? What was Demas before this? Compare this Scripture with the Epistle to the Colossians, and you shall see what he was before this. He was an ardent disciple of Paul's, and the apostle held him in high esteem. Read Colossians 4:14, where Paul was directed by the Holy Ghost to say, "Luke, the beloved physician, and Demas greet you." Paul ranks Demas here among the famous professors of religion. The apostle, writing to the Colossians, said, "Demas greets you among the rest." When we write to our friends and say, "Such and such a one commends him to you," we usually do not name them unless they are good friends.

The interpreters think it was the same Demas, and the word gives some ground for this. In Timothy, you find that he names Luke there, too. It seems that Demas and Luke were two great associates. Paul mentions them together. When Demas had forsaken him, Luke still rode with him, and when Paul sends them the greetings of Luke, the beloved physician, he sends the greetings of Demas, too. But one was truly godly and, whatever sufferings Paul met with, one cleaved to him and would not forsake him.

But when Paul began to suffer, Demas thought, "There's no thriving for me if I follow this persecuted apostle." Demas would have no more of Paul; he thanked him for his company and departed from him. "He hath forsaken me." What's the reason? "He has embraced this present world."

Another note: though he was an ardent professor, Paul's heart was not very affectionate towards him, for he said, "Luke, the beloved physician, and Demas greet you." He did not say "the beloved Demas." It's true, Demas was an ardent professor, and he seemed to wear a cloak of religion, yet Paul was directed by the Holy Ghost only to speak of him as a professor.

The Holy Ghost directs Paul to speak of the two as companions together, giving one an epithet, "beloved," while only giving the other's name. Two men, both very ardent, and companions together, yet those who are godly, old disciples can savor one more than the other. They are both professors, and both have excellent parts and gifts, yet there's more spirituality and greater experiences in one than in the other; for it appears that there was more in Luke than in Demas. Your earthly-minded men afterwards prove to be apostates. Usually, before their grand apostasy, they manifest some deadness and waywardness of spirit to that which is good. Yes, their spirits reveal them to be earthly spirits. They smell of the earth.

Before a man dies, his breath will smell very earthy. You will say, "Oh, such a one cannot live; his breath is so earthy!" So it is with those who are great professors of religion. Those who have an intimate acquaintance with them before they apostatize smell their breath to be earthly in their duties, in their conferences. Oh, take heed of earthly-mindedness lest it be the root of apostasy. This may be written on an apostate's grave, "THIS WAS AN EARTHLY-MINDED MAN OR WOMAN IN SPITE OF THEIR PROFESSION." And hence it is that they fell from the truth in times of danger. When they were brought to the trial, they were base backsliders from God and His truth.

THE NINTH EVIL. Earthly-mindedness wonderfully deadens the heart in prayer. It sinks the spirits of men and straitens them out in spiritual duties. Indeed, it defiles every duty of religion. In Psalm 119:37, David prays to God that He would turn away his eyes from beholding vanity, and that He would quicken him in His Law. Certainly, the vanity of which he speaks there means the things of the world; and by his eyes he means the eyes of the mind, chiefly working on the thoughts of his heart after earthly things.

If you look at verse 36, he says, "Incline my heart to Thy testimonies," and not to covetousness. "O Lord, let not my heart be inclined to covetousness; turn away my eyes from beholding vanity, so that my heart may not be inclined to covetousness. Lord, let not my thoughts be busied with such vain things, but quicken me in Thy law." It is as if he were to say, "Lord, while my mind is turned to vanity or my heart to covetousness after the things of the earth, I always find my spirit dull and heavy in any holy duties. I have no quickness at all in my inward man when I come into Thy presence, and, by experience, I find this to be the reason that my heart is so drossy, because my thoughts and mind are set on earthly things that are vain." Therefore, "Lord, let not mine heart be inclined to covetousness, nor mine eyes after vanity, but turn away mine eyes from these things and quicken me in Thy Law."

If you would have your hearts quickened in God's law, in the duties that God sets you on, take heed of your eyes that they look not after vanity, and your hearts that they follow not after covetousness, for an earthly spirit will be a dead spirit. As the dust of the earth is the most sluggish, dead element of all, so earthliness in the heart makes the heart sluggish, dead, and lifeless to any holy and spiritual duty. I appeal to your consciences in this. When you have let your hearts out after the things of this earth, and have been exercised in the world and in business, then when you have come to have communion with God, oh, how dead have you found your hearts! A drossy heart must be a dead heart in heavenly exercises.

You complain many times of your vain thoughts in the performance of holy duties. You cry out of dead spirits then, but here lies the cause: you have given yourselves up so much to the things of the world at other times that, when you come to converse with God, your hearts are so dead and dull. This is the ground of it; this is the great root of all, it lies here in your earthly-mindedness. Oh, how many prayers have been spoiled by an earthly heart! Whereas those who have spiritual hearts have enjoyed blessed communion with God at the throne of His grace, and have been sweetly refreshed, while you have gone with a dead heart and continued there, and come away with a dead heart without any quickness and life. This is that which comes by your earthly-mindedness, which is such a restraint to duties.

THE TENTH EVIL. Earthly-mindedness is so great an evil, wherever it prevails, that it would be just of God that your name should be written in the earth. Those who are earthly-minded and have this prevailing upon their hearts, and who are not sensible of it, have cause to fear God lest He should write their names in the dust, yea, lest God already has written their names in the earth. In Jeremiah 17: 13, we read such an expression: "O Lord, the hope of Israel, all that forsake Thee shall be ashamed, and they that depart from Thee shall be written in the earth, because they have forsaken the Lord, the fountain of living waters." It's apparent that he speaks of earthly spirits here, for in the 11th verse he says, "As the partridge sitteth on eggs and hatcheth them not, so he that getteth riches, and not by right, shall leave them in the midst of his days, and at his end shall be a fool."

Then he goes on to describe the excellency of God and His sanctuary: "A glorious high throne from the beginning is the place of our sanctuary," and so forth. It is as if he should say that there is a company of foolish, vain men who seek after nothing but getting richer in the things of the earth, "but a glorious high throne from the beginning is the place of Thy sanctuary." That is to say, "O Lord, we see an excellency in Thee, in Thine ordinances, and in Thy sanctuary. O Lord, the hope of Israel, in whom there is such excellency, is there any who forsake Thee, who has so much excellency in Thyself, who are the hope of Israel? O Lord, it would be just that their names should be written in the earth, that they should never come to partake of those good things that are in Thee, the excellent things that are in Thine ordinances, and in thy gospel. But, Lord, let their names be written in the earth; let God write concerning such a man or woman, 'EARTH SHALL BE THEIR PORTION.' "

Their mouths shall be filled with earth one day, and that's all the good they shall have from the Almighty. Oh, those who have known God and the things of eternal life cannot but apprehend this to be a sad and grievous evil, to have their name written in the earth!

THE ELEVENTH EVIL. An earthly-minded man has the curse of the serpent upon him. What is that? "Upon thy belly shalt thou go, and dust shalt thou eat." You have the curse of the serpent; you grovel upon the earth, as it were, upon your belly. Your soul cleaves to the ground in a sinful way, and you feed upon dust. While the saints are feeding upon Jesus Christ, upon the very flesh and blood of Christ, refreshing themselves with the hidden manna, angels' bread, corn from heaven, you satiate yourself with the earth. That's your food, and that's the very curse of the serpent. It's a sign of a serpentine brood, and of the old serpent, to be groveling upon the earth and to feed upon it.

THE TWELFTH EVIL. Earthly-mindedness is a dishonor to God and a scandal to religion. What, do you profess an interest in Christ, and are there no higher things to be had in God than the base things your heart is set upon? What, do you hold forth the everlasting gospel in your hand to others, and openly profess to be nearer to God than others, and is there no difference between the workings of your heart and the workings of others after the things of this world? Oh, how this darkens the excellency of grace! If there is any grace at all, it very much clouds it. Like the mixing of earth and drossy stuff with pure metal takes away the excellency of the pure metal, so the mixing of the earth with the profession of religion blemishes the beauty and splendor of the profession of religion.

You will never be the man or woman who is likely to convince any by your conversation; you are never likely to be a means to draw any to the love of the ways of godliness, because there is so much darkness and earthliness in your conversation. "Oh," they will say, "indeed he or she makes a great blaze in the world, and talks much of religion and ordinances and such things; but they are as worldly as any and groveling in the earth as much as any." People who are bystanders will think that profession is but a mere verbal thing, a pretense, when they see as much earthliness in your conversation as in the conversation of those who are without any profession of religion. You bring a bad report upon the things of God, as did the spies about the land of Canaan.

Every professor of religion should endeavor to put a luster on religion, and to make the ways of God to be beautiful, amiable, and glorious in the eyes of all who behold them. But to give a lie about a gospel profession by your earthly conversation is a very great scandal to the name of Christ that is upon you, and to His gospel that you seem to stand up for! Oh, there's a great evil in this, and a very bad report comes upon the ways of religion by this. Many who have had little religion in them have some kind of generosity of spirit, so that they scorn such base sordidness as some professors are given to. Oh, for shame! Let not those who have only common gifts of nature and education outstrip you who seem to be the followers of Christ. Away with that base, muddy, earthy, saving, pinching disposition. It becomes none but Judas, who carried the bag and betrayed his Lord and Master for eighteen shillings and four pence.

Let me argue with you who have to deal with friends or neighbors who you are afraid do not have the power of godliness in them that you desire. You see they have much ingenuity, generosity, and a concern for the public good. Take heed of scandalizing such men, for certainly if such men could be brought to the love of religion, to the power and strictness thereof, had they the work of the Holy Ghost upon their hearts to humble them for sin, and to show the excellency of Jesus Christ, they would be glorious instruments in the church of God and the commonwealth. Therefore, it's a very great evil to scandalize such men as these. No, you should labor to walk so that they might see a beauty and excellency in the ways of religion by your conversation. Oh, it would be a thousand times better for you to be cut short of the things of this world than that you should scandalize the ways of God, and the profession of the name and gospel of Jesus Christ!

THE THIRTEENTH EVIL. Earthly-mindedness exceedingly hinders preparation for death, and it is likely to make death very grievous and terrible when it comes. "Take heed to yourselves," Christ said to His disciples, "lest any time your hearts be overcharged or filled with indulgence and drunkenness and cares of this life." Note how He puts them all together. It's very strange, you might say, that Christ should say this to His disciples, to forewarn them of this. We do not think that they were drunkards, following after taverns or alehouses, or reeling in the streets. But by this drunkenness, He means any excessive use of meat or drink; and professors of religion may be subject to that, to give themselves up too much to sensual delights and excess in the use of the creature.

But besides that, though there are many who would abhor gluttony and drunkenness, yet the cares of this life take up their hearts. Therefore Christ said, "Take heed to yourselves lest at any time your hearts be overcharged with the cares of this life." Why? What evil would come from filling the heart with the cares of this life? Mark, says the text, "And so that day will come upon you unawares. For as a snare shall it come upon all them that dwell upon the face of the whole earth. Watch ye therefore, and pray always."

I may apply this to death, though the Scripture is speaking of Christ's coming. In the time of death, Christ comes particularly. There is a particular day of judgment at the day of death. It may likewise be applied to the time of any affliction. Then the evil of earthly-mindedness appears in that it hinders the preparation of the soul for affliction. Oh, earthly-mindedness will make your affliction grievous and heavy to you! An affliction is a very grievous thing to an earthly spirit. If God comes to take away any comforts of this world because your heart cleaves so closely to them, there must be a rending of them from you, and that will put you to pain.

A man who wears loose garments can easily put them off when he goes to bed at night; but if a man has a sore upon his body, and his inward garments cleave to the sore, when he pulls them off, it puts him to a great deal of pain. Oh, then he cries out in his pain! Truly, this earthly-mindedness comes from distemper of spirit, and the things of the earth cleave to the hearts of men and women that are earthly like the inward garment would cleave to a sore on a man's body.

Now, when afflictions or death come to take away the things of the earth from them, or them from the things of the earth, it's painful and grievous to them. For one who has an earthly spirit, it's a hundred to one against him having any light of conscience left in him. But his conscience will trouble him in time of sickness, and then tell him how he has spent his time and strength of spirit on the things of the earth, when they should have been spent on more excellent things.

When he comes to die, then, his spirit will be troubled thusly, "I am now to leave all these things that I have spent my care and thoughts on and let my heart go after, and what good is it to me now? What good is it that I shall leave so much more than my neighbor does? What great content is this to me when I am upon my sick and deathbed? What comfort can I have in all the good things I have enjoyed? Yea, through the earthliness of my spirit, I have enjoyed little of them, yet I have troublesome thoughts. But now death is likely to be to me as a strainer, that strains out the good and leaves the dross and the dirt behind it. So all the good of the things of the world is gone, but the guiltiness that I have contracted upon my spirit with my immoderate care and affections is now upon my spirit."

I remember a man who lived in a place not far from where I formerly lived, who had a covetous, earthly spirit. When he was about to die, he called for his money and fell to swearing, "Must I leave you now?" He was speaking to his bags of money and hugging them! What! "Must I leave you now?" Here was an earthly man who had spent his spirits and strength upon these things, and indeed, let out his heart to them as his portion. Then he saw that he must be stripped of all. He must bid an eternal farewell to all—no more houses, no lands, nor money. Oh, death is grievous to such a man!

Now, what should the life of a Christian be but a continual preparation for death? Many of the heathens said of philosophy that it was but a preparation for death. It is a special excellency of Christianity that it is a preparative for death; and therefore you should let out your hearts to the things of this world, and be continually thinking of death, so that when God calls you to part from these things, you may do it with as much ease as a man who is going to bed casts off his loose clothes. The grave is a bed to the saints where they fall asleep when they die, and so they may lay down all things and go to their sleep with ease and peace.

A man or woman can have their consciences tell them, "I have been diligent in my calling, but God knows through faithfulness to Him rather than love to the world. And I have kept my heart close to God and faithful to Him. I can bid the world farewell now. As the world has done with me, so I have done with it. So long as my time was to work for God, God continued those things that this frail nature of mine needed. Now my work is done; farewell to the comforts of this world. I expect other comforts where I am going." Such a one who is spiritual may die with comfort, but those who have their hearts filled with the cares of this life will have the day of Christ come upon them unawares.

THE FOURTEENTH EVIL. Earthly-mindedness is that which will bring destruction at last, as it will drown your soul in perdition. There are two texts for it. The first is here in this text. The apostle says here, speaking of men who mind earthly things, that their end is destruction. He joins both together: earthly-mindedness will bring destruction at last. And the other passage for our purposes is 1 Timothy 6:9, where the apostle speaks of bringing them into snares and foolish lusts, "which drown men in destruction and perdition." Some who are washing themselves in the Thames River go a little way at first, and then venture a little further and further, and at length, they are over their heads and ears. There they are drowned and cannot recover themselves. So it will be with your hearts if you do not look after them.

You think you may venture so far to the things of this world. Why? Are they not good and in themselves lawful? "I did not get my estate by wrongdoing or cheating." And so by degrees your hearts are stolen away from God and are taken with these earthly things. You get deeper and deeper into the world until, at length, you are plunged in over your head and ears before you are aware, and then you cannot recover yourselves. That man who gives his heart to the things of this world and thinks that he will go no further, I bet a hundred to one that once these things have taken up his heart, he gets more and more advantage, until this man is drowned in destruction and perdition.

A man or woman may be undone as much by earthliness, and be damned and perish eternally, as by adultery, drunkenness, murder, or any notorious sin. Many who are great professors of religion, it's very likely that the earthliness of their minds will be the sin by which they will perish to all eternity. Do not deceive yourselves into thinking that because you keep from those gross and notorious sins that others live in, therefore you hope to be saved. Your earthliness may damn you as well as anything else. Upon dunghills, you cast not only carrion and such nasty stuff, but the dust that you sweep from your houses. I may compare hell, which is the place where God casts those damned out of His presence, to the common dunghill upon which filthy creatures are cast. Now upon that dunghill there are not only carrions and filthy blasphemers, whore-masters and thieves, but there will also be dust upon that dunghill, and scrapings from your houses cast upon the dunghill of hell from the presence of God. Therefore, do not satisfy yourselves that you do not lie in such filthy, abominable lusts as others do. If you have foul, earthly hearts, you may be cast upon the dunghill as well as those who have lived most notoriously wicked. Therefore take heed of earthly-mindedness.

There is a great deal of evil and danger in earthly-mindedness, may the Lord keep us from it. I shall enlarge my meditations upon this subject by opening some proofs, to further convince men and women that there is a great deal of earthly-mindedness in them. And for preparation, I will lay this down. First, a man or woman may be earthly-minded, and yet little think of it themselves, not knowing that they are so. Yea, and it may be even perish eternally through their earthly-mindedness, and not know it of themselves.

CHAPTER FIVE

Nine Proofs of Earthly-Mindedness

There are five things that may be true of a man, and yet he may still be earthly-minded:

1. A man may be convinced that there is vanity in all the things of this world and yet be an earthly-minded man. Many think they are not earthly-minded. Why? Because they are convinced that all these things are vanity. Come and speak to them about the things of this world and they will acknowledge that there is a vanity in all these things, that they are vanity of vanities, and that all is vanity.

2. A man may have some kind of contentment in his estate and yet have an earthly mind, as in Genesis 33:9. Esau was one of the earth. He said he had enough, yet he was certainly one of an earthly spirit; and his portion was in the earth. How many of you have come as far as did Esau, to say of your estates that you have enough? Oh, 'tis a shame for those who are professors of religion, and would seem to be of the seed of Jacob, to not be able to say they have enough, when an Esau can say that he has enough.

3. Men and women may speak very great words about the vanity of all the things of this world. When you come to converse, you may discourse much about them and yet have a very earthly spirit.

4. A man may be free from getting anything of this world by false means, by deceit, by injustice, and the like, and yet be earthly for all that.

5. Through some predominant lust for something else, a man may seem to despise some earthly thing. For example, many men who have a lust for ambition will seem to despise money. Those who have a lust to show themselves generous, and those who have a lust of sensuality, will seem to despise the things of the world. Many a man, through one lust, will seem as if he hates the other; but the truth is he does not hate it as sin but because it is opposite to some other lust that he has. He does not hate it; he has no dislike of it as a sin against God. Your prodigals, your young spendthrifts, speak against covetousness as if they hated that sin, whereas the truth is that no wicked man hates any sin any further than one sin crosses another. He may hate it, but not as a sin.

In Isaiah 13:17, the text says, "I will stir up the Medes against them, which shall not regard silver, and as for gold they shall not delight in it." The Medes were heathen, wicked people who had no grace in them at all; and yet the text says that they shall not regard silver nor delight in gold. Some men think it is through the work of grace because they find that they are above the base covetousness they see in other men. They do not regard silver and gold, or getting all for themselves, and they despise those men who are of such a base, covetous way. Upon that they think that their condition is good because they think they are above that lust. But you see it is no different than a Mede. A heathen may disregard silver and gold, but how? It is because his spirit is upon another lust; that's the ground of it.

Can you say this, you who seem to scorn covetousness, and hate such base sordidness as you see in some men, "The Lord has made me to know what communion with Himself in Jesus Christ means; and since that time I bless God that my heart has been above all these earthly things. And that's the reason that I look upon all these earthly things as vanity, because the Lord has revealed to me those excellent and glorious things that are infinitely above these earthly things."

That's something, indeed. If you can be above earthliness on this ground, that's a good argument! Therefore, examine upon what ground it is that your spirit is against such things, whether it is upon the sight and experience of better things. If so, then it's right. But certainly men and women may go far in seeming to be above earthly things in respect to the sin of covetousness, and still have earthly minds. Now I will proceed to give you arguments, besides those things to which I have hinted.

How does a man value himself and others? Is it not because those others, or yourselves, have much of the things of the earth? Can you value a poor man who is godly above the richest man who is wicked? And so, can you value yourselves for the least work of grace upon your hearts to make you more excellent than the greatest gathering of your estates? But at these things we have already hinted.

And then, where lies the chief joy and sorrow of men's hearts? What is it that most troubles your hearts? Is it the loss of the light of the face of God, or the loss of an estate; the loss of a voyage, or the commission of a sin? What's your chief joy, your profiting from the Word or gaining from a bargain? You have come to the Word and, sometimes, God has there revealed some truth to you, and you have profited. Can you go away rejoicing because God has made you to know His Law? "The Lord has darted some truth into my soul this morning. Oh! I will go away rejoicing, and my heart is filled with more joy than I've ever had from some bargain." These are two proofs at which we had not hinted before.

NINE PROOFS OF EARTHLY-MINDEDNESS

1. Seriously consider this: when a man rests upon earthly props, upon worldly helps for the good that he expects, if he can have those things, his heart seems to be upon the wing; he is very pleasant. But there is nothing else that can revive his heart, nothing else that can keep his spirit. Now that which a man or woman most trusts in, they have made to be their god. It properly belongs to God to put our trust in Him. We make God, then, to be our God when we roll ourselves upon Him. You will say, "I cannot trust in earthly things to bring me to God." No, but to trust in them for the comforts of this life while you are here in this world is an argument of an earthly spirit for, the truth is, the comfort of a man's life consists not in any earthly thing that he might enjoy.

OBJECTION: You will say, "Do not these things make our lives more comfortable?"
ANSWER: Yes, so far as God is pleased to let Himself out through them, but if your heart rests on these for comfort, and does not look higher than these for comfort, even for outward support, certainly you have an earthly heart. And so, when you are about any business, you have some earthly means to further you.

OBJECTION: You will say, "God would have us to take all outward means to help us."

ANSWER: Aye, but not to trust in anything. If riches increase, do not set your hearts upon them. If friends increase, do not set your hearts upon them, but trust in the living God. Let it be the living God whom you rest on for all outward things in this world.

2. A second proof is when men make most provision for the things of this world, both for themselves and for their children. Are these not your thoughts? I do not know what I may want hereafter, and I see many who have lived finely when they have been young yet, afterwards, they have lived miserably, and therefore I must make provision for aftertimes. But now, do you reason thus for the things of heaven? Do not I see many that have made a great blaze of religion, and yet afterwards they have come to nothing? They have gone out in a snuff as men that God has forsaken, and they have died in horror of conscience. Therefore, let me lay up provision now against an evil time so that I may not miscarry in the matters of my soul as others have done. This is a sign that your minds are not earthly.

God has sent you children and, oh, how you toil and labor! Your thoughts run in the night, and as soon as you wake in the morning, about what you shall get for their portions, and an estate for them. Now I appeal to your consciences before God, the Searcher of all hearts. Have your cares been to provide in a suitable way for their souls, for their spiritual and eternal estates? There is no question but that it's lawful for parents to provide in a providential way for their children, and they that do not are worse than infidels. But what is your chief provision for? Are your thoughts more solicitous to provide portions for them, than that they should have instructions in the fear of God, an interest in Christ, grace wrought in their hearts? You are loath to die before you can bring your estate to its fullness so you may leave it to your children. Are you not loath to die before such a time as you can see some work of grace wrought in the heart of your children? These would be your thoughts if you were spiritual!

Augustine's mother said, "Oh, could I discern just some seeds of grace sown before I was dissolved, I could rejoice abundantly!" The great thing she desired to live for was to see her son converted. God granted her desire, and then she found herself willing to die. There's nothing that will make the spiritual heart of a father or mother more willing to depart from this world, than to find grace wrought in their children. "Oh, that I may see before I die, my child left under the promise in covenant with God." But those whose cares and thoughts are mostly for these earthly things, in providing for themselves and their children, give proof that their hearts are earthly.

3. A third proof (which is very notable, and I beseech you all to lay this to heart and consider it seriously) of the evil of this earthly-mindedness is that it is a very secret and close sin. Therefore I am going to be longer in this point.

The proof is this: that man who can be content with a slight assurance in the matters of heaven, except for the matters of earth, never thinks himself sure enough. But he is very careful to make all things so infallible that there can be no way he can be deceived, that he may surely build upon what he has in the things of the earth. This is proof of an earthly mind. Come to men that are earthly and talk with them about matters that concern their souls. "What evidence have you that you are gone beyond any formal professor, that you are better than the stony ground that we read of in Scripture? What evidence have you that the saving work of grace is wrought in you? That you have shot the gulf? That you are translated out of the kingdom of darkness into the kingdom of Jesus Christ? And that your sins are pardoned and your souls justified? That you are at peace with God? What evidences do you have of peace made between God and your soul?"

This answer would be given, "I hope I am converted. I trust in God's mercy. I am sure I have grace. I shall be saved, for God is merciful." But what evidences can they show? They scarcely know any. You will have many like that, because they do not know what assurance means, therefore they will think nobody can be assured. We may hope well, but we cannot come to be assured of it.

A heart that is truly gracious and godly would loathe that to be true. They would not lose their part in the blessings of assurance for a thousand worlds, even if God were to make them kings or queens of the earth. But you have an earthly, drossy heart, and do not look much after assurance for matters of your soul and eternal estate. You will venture those matters and put them upon chance. But when it comes to the matters of the earth you'll make sure there, and go from this lawyer to that lawyer for counsel. If there is anything you can do to be more sure, you will do it. If you could but hear of anything your neighbors had done to be more certain than you, you would not even rest until you had done as much. Is it so in matters of your eternal estate?

Do you not hear of many saints of God who walk comfortably in the midst of all afflictions upon the assurance of God's love? You will have some who will be able to say, "Aye, and it's this Scripture I build upon and, through God's mercy, such has been the work of God upon my soul in revealing Himself to me, and such a promise I have sucked an abundance of honey from." But now, come to people upon their sick beds, and, generally, all they say is that they hope in God's mercy. But for the ground of hope, for showing how God has been pleased to bring their hearts and the Word together, and what real effects there have been upon their spirits by the Word, they can show nothing. You have, therefore, not gotten that assurance for your soul and eternal estate as others have, and yet you can go on quietly.

Oh, it concerns you who are so busy in making all sure for your outward estate, to spend more thoughts and care in the matters of your soul and eternal estate than ever you have done. Here's an earthly-minded man that can be contented with slight assurance for the matters of his soul, and be satisfied with no kind of assurance in the matters of the world but would make those things more and more sure continually.

4. Further, an earthly-minded man may be convinced of his earthliness in this, that he is content with a little degree of sanctification, but regarding the matters of the world, he would have more and more. He looks at those that are the most eminent in his rank, and he would get as high as they are in the things of this life. But in matters of religion, he looks at the lowest Christians and is content to be as low as they are.

Take an earthly-minded man that is of such and such a trade. If there is anyone of his profession or calling that had as little to begin with as he, and was thriving better, he would desire to get that high himself, and he is troubled that he is not as rich. That's how it is in the world.

But now, take them in matters of God. There are such men who began when you began, and had as little means for the good of their souls as you have had, who have thrived and gone beyond you abundantly in the matters of God. Does this trouble you? Are your thoughts solicitous about this?

Do you say, "Oh, that I could attain to the degree of grace that man has, for he has a spiritual mind, and is full of the joy of the Holy Ghost! He is full of faith, he is able to depend upon

God in the lack of all outward comforts, and certainly enjoys much communion with God, but I am far beneath him." Do these thoughts trouble you? It is ordinary for earthly spirits to look upon the lowest Christian and be satisfied that they are like them, but for the matters of the world they look upon the highest, and are not satisfied unless they attain to that level. That's a fourth evidence.

5. A fifth proof is this: earthly-minded men are very wise in matters of the world, but in matters that are spiritual are very weak and simple. You have many men who, in matters of religion, are very ignorant. If they do speak in points of saving knowledge, they speak like children, so that one would wonder where their understandings were. Now turn such men to the matters of the world. Oh, how wise they are in their generation. How subtle and crafty are they! They can see an objection there and know how to answer it. They can discern anything that will let them see a profit many miles off. But in those things that hinder their souls, they cannot see things there. They are wise in their generation and have memories for the matters of the world. They can understand things and remember things, and they can meditate there, but put them to meditate upon a point of religion, they come to a standstill. Let me appeal to you. Do not your consciences tell you? In worldly matters, when you are walking from here to London, you can run your thoughts on business all the way. You can plot this and contrive that. You can foresee this objection and that one, and you can answer each one in you own thoughts. But let me put this to you. When you walk through the fields, settle upon one meditation about Christ and see whether you are able to draw out that meditation the entire time you walk, whereas you can spin out an earthly meditation no matter how far your journey is. When you awake in the night, your thoughts are upon the things of the world,

and you can draw them out and work with understanding, but how about the things of God? Oh, how barren and simple are you there! There is scarcely anyone who can outdo you in the things of the world, but in the matters of religion you are outdone; every slight temptation overcomes you there.

6. Besides this, you may know earthly-mindedness by the discourse and words of men. I John 4:5 says, "They are of the world, therefore they speak of the world, and the world heareth them." Their breath is earthly. Oh, it's an ill sign that when you come to a friend's bedside and fear that they will die because their breath smells so earthy. It's a symptom of the death of their bodies. So your hearts smell earthy, and it would be somewhat tolerable if it were only on the days when your calling requires you to talk about business. But even during that time that God has set apart for Himself, you are often discoursing in your own thoughts about the business of the world. You do it when you are praying; you do it when you are hearing the Word. The communication and discourses of men should relish what they have heard out of the Word, not go and talk about some earthly occurrences.

Oh, it's this that has lost many precious truths. It may have been when you have been hearing the Word, God has darted some beam of gospel light into your souls, and you have lost it before you got home, and have come to lose the impression of the truth you have heard. Oh, what a seemly thing it is that those who come to hear the Word depart with no discourse about what they have heard! Oh, how often are you in company and never leave anything to refresh one another's spirits, or to further one another in the way to eternal life! Though God gives you allowance to speak about your business, yet still, if you are spiritual and heavenly, He would have you to have something of eternal life before you depart.

7. A further proof is this: when spiritual things must give way to earthliness upon every little business. Prayer must pay for it. If I have any business to do, I will take it out of prayer time, or converse in the Word the less, or hear the Word less. When earthly things are as high as spiritual things, heaven must stand by until earth is served. This is an evil sign of an earthly spirit. Whereas, were the spirit heavenly, the very first thing that you would do when you awake in the morning would be to season your heart with something that is spiritual.

In Psalm 139:17–18, we read, "How precious also are Thy thoughts unto me, O God! How great is the sum of them! If I count them, they are more in number than the sand, when I awake I am still with Thee." That is an argument of a spiritual mind, to be with God upon awaking, "When I am awake I am still with Thee." But now I appeal to you, who are you with when you awake? Can you say, "Lord, when I awake I am still with Thee. I find an inclination in my spirit to be upon the matters of heaven, and when I am up, I would rather my worldly business give way than my spiritual duties."

8. When a man or woman does not care how it is with the church, with the kingdom of Jesus Christ, as long as it is well with them in matters of the world, this is proof of an earthly mind. When things are stirring abroad in the world, he does not inquire how things are in respect to the privileges of the saints, the ark of the church, as long as his cabin is safe. Truly, there is nothing needed but the examining of your own hearts, how they have been these last years of Jacob's troubles. In the time of war, Eli sat trembling because of the Ark of God. He did not sit trembling because the Philistines might prevail and take his home. No, it was because of the Ark of God. That was proof of the spirituality of Eli's mind.

Likewise, it may be an argument of great comfort to you

in these dangerous times if your consciences tell you this, that God, who knows all things, knows that the great thing your heart was solicitous in these evil days was, "What shall become of Thy great name? Lord, what shall become of religion? What shall become of the gospel? Lord, these were the things that took up my heart, not so much what should become of my estate and outward accommodations and relations in this world".

Oh, examine your hearts in this, whether the care of your spirits is more for the furtherance of the kingdom of Jesus Christ or for the furtherance of your estates! But for that man or woman who is most solicitous about the business of his or her outward estate, and does not much care how religion goes, or how the way of the kingdom of Christ is maintained, God at this time speaks to that soul.

You are an earthly-minded man or woman and, therefore, take heed lest what has been spoken concerning the great evil there is in earthly-mindedness befalls you, and especially these words, "whose end is destruction, who art drowned in perdition"; lest hereafter this is the thing that you shall lie crying out and cursing yourself for. "Oh, I had a base and earthly heart, and sought the things of the earth. I made my portion there, and in the meantime, the blessed God has been forsaken. I have lost my portion in the Holy Land, for I had my portion in Egypt among the Egyptians, according as I chose for myself."

9. The more spiritual any truth is that is revealed, the less it takes with his heart. Some truths of religion move him, perhaps, but these are as bywords to him, he does not mind them at all. The more spiritual an ordinance is, the less his spirit is moved by it. If he comes to the Word and there is some earthly, natural excellence mingled there—like natural parts, wisdom, wit, eloquence, and learning—that will move him. It may be

that some fine story is more pleasing to him than the goodly pearls of truth that are revealed in the Word, like the enjoyment of communion with God, the longing after Jesus Christ's coming, the living by faith upon a bare promise, the excellency that there is in suffering for Jesus Christ. These truths are spiritual, the mortifying of the inward lusts, self-denial. These things are favored but little by an earthly-minded man.

Tell him of the privileges of the saints, the mysteries of the gospel. Anything that is spiritual is but a notion to him. As it is with men that are upon the earth, they look up to heaven and see the things of heaven only slightly. Why is it that the stars seem so small to us here? It is because we are on the earth. The earth seems a vast body to us, but the stars seem little to us, even though they are far bigger than the earth. Were we in heaven, the heavenly bodies would seem vast to us, and the earthly bodies would scarcely be discerned by us. Were men's hearts heavenly, all the things of the earth would seem little to them, but because they are earthly, the things of heaven and spiritual mysteries are very small in their eyes.

CHAPTER SIX

Seven Reasons of Men's Earthly-Mindedness

I shall now proceed to the reasons why it is that men's hearts are so set upon the earth, minding earthly things. Briefly, I will give you these reasons for it.

First, the things of the earth appear real to them, but spiritual and heavenly things are just a notion. That which has reality in it takes most with the heart. Men are deceived in this, though, for the Scripture speaks of spiritual things as the only real things, and earthly things as those that have no being at all. In Proverbs 23:5 it says, "Wilt thou set thine eyes upon that which is not?" (speaking of the riches of the world); it has no reality in it at all. But in Proverbs 8:20–21, "Lead me in the way of righteousness, in the midst of the paths of judgment, that I may cause those that love me to inherit substance"—to inherit that which is, that which has a being. The honors of the earth are but a fantasy and vain show. You have read of Bernice and Agrippa. They came with much pomp, with great fancy, as the original says. But to an earthly man, these earthly things are real things, and therefore he minds them. Wisdom is a lie to a fool.

Second, they look upon these things as necessary, though the Scripture tells us but of one thing that is necessary. Yet they think that these earthly things are present now, they only have need of heavenly things hereafter. They may have need of reconciliation with God, pardon of sin, peace of conscience, and such things. They may have need of them, that is, when they depart out of this life. Oh, the infinite folly of most hearts to think that there is so present a necessity of spiritual and heavenly things, whereas indeed, our life consists in them for the present! This is eternal life. We may come here in this world to enjoy eternal life, but the majority of people look upon all spiritual things only as our good for the future, when we leave here and are seen no more.

Third, these things are most suitable to men's hearts. It's no wonder that they mind earthly things, they are of the earth, and from the earth; they have nothing but the first Adam in them. The first man was from the earth earthly. The truth is, the happiness of man's estate even in innocence, in the morning of the day of his creation, in comparison of the things that are now revealed by the gospel, was but earthly.

Take man when he was in paradise; that paradise was but earthly. But then take man in his fallen and corrupt estate. He cannot help but be earthly, and everything closes with what is suitable to that. Comfort does not come so much from the goodness of a thing, but from the suitableness of the object with the faculty. Now the things of the earth are suitable to men that are of the earth, and therefore they mind them. The heart will abundantly run out upon that which is suitable to it.

Fourth, these things of the earth have a very fair show in the flesh. They have a kind of goodly appearance in the eye of sense, and in the eye of that reason that is now corrupted by sin. We have a most elegant expression of these earthly things, and those earthly-minded men who have their hearts set upon these things. It is in Galatians 6:12. "As many as desire to make a fair show in the flesh," says the Scripture. The words are to signify when a man looks smug and neat. You shall have some men that dress themselves curiously and, having handsome bodies, they look so trim, fine, handsome, and very splendid to the eyes of all who behold them. So, he says, these men that are false teachers desire to make a fair show in the flesh. That is, they look upon the things of the flesh as those things that are appealing to the eye, and they look to have all things so complete about them so that they may look smug, and carry themselves with such beauty before the world.

Oh, this is their happiness; this they take satisfaction in! They seem to have fine estates, and to have appealing clothing, and all curious things about them. This looks so good in the eyes of the world, and therefore it is that their hearts are upon them. They are here enemies to the cross of Christ. They think suffering for Christ, poverty, or disgrace looks bad. But now, those that desire to make a fair show in the flesh, that would have their countenances well washed, fair, and beautiful wherever they go, and be somebody in this world, forsake the truths of God and seek to provide for themselves in the things of the flesh.

Fifth, men naturally never knew better things than the things of the earth. It is no marvel, therefore, that they mind the things of the earth so much. Children that are born in a dungeon and never knew any better place can play up and down in the dungeon. So it is with men that never knew what the things of heaven and eternal life meant. They can mind earthly things better than those, but when the Lord opens the eyes of their understanding to see into the reality, excellency, and glory of spiritual things, then they wonder at their former blindness in minding such poor, low, mean, foolish rattles, as the things of the earth are.

Sixth, there are earthly principles continually dropped into men by conversing with other earthly men. Psalm 49:11: "Their inward thoughts are that their houses shall continue forever, and their dwelling place to all generations; they call their lands after their own names." Their hearts are set on earthly things. Then in verse 13: "Their way is folly, yet their posterity approves their sayings." They are applauded by men. They see that everybody applauds them in these ways, and when they converse with one another, they converse about the things of the earth. They see everybody following the things of the earth, and they are greedy after these toys. That also inclines their minds to the things of the earth.

Last, the sensible experience they have had of the sweetness there is in the things of the earth takes their minds off spiritual things, and makes them to mind the things of the earth. But though these are the reasons why men mind the things of the earth, someday it will be shown to be folly. Though an earthly-minded man blesses himself in this way, and thinks he has good reason for what he does, and thinks all men fools who do not grovel in the ground like a mole with him, and look upon the matters of religion as mere words and talk, let them do what they will, I will find contentment here. Their way will be proven folly. As the Holy Ghost said in Psalm 49: "Their way is folly."

In the end, the wise men of the earth, those that have sought the things of the earth and bless themselves in their way, will prove to be the greatest fools; the Holy Ghost accounts them so. Jeremiah 17:11: "As the partridge sitteth on eggs and hatcheth them not, so he that getteth riches and not by right, shall leave them in the midst of his days, and at his end shall be a fool." He applauds himself for what he presently has, but at the end he shall be a fool.

CHAPTER SEVEN

Eleven Considerations to Take the Mind Off of Earthly-Mindedness

The main thing we have tried to do thus far is to take the minds of men and women off of the things of the earth. This will prepare us for the next point that is of infinite concern, our conversations in heaven. But because a man's conversation cannot be in heaven until his mind is taken off of the earth, until the disease of earthly-mindedness is cured, we must now propound those things that may help take off men's minds from the earth.

First consider this: if you could possess all the things of the earth that your mind and heart are upon, there is still not enough good in them as to undo the evil of the least sin, not the least sin of thought. Your heart is muddling upon the earth, and you think that you would be blessed if you had thus and thus as others have. Let me tell you if you had but one sinful thought, there is more evil in that than there is good in all that you shall get all the days of your life. And, if this is so, it concerns you rather to have your mind on how to avoid sin, how to get the evil of sin removed, and how to get your sin mortified.

That ought to concern you more than minding and plodding about the things of the earth. That's one consideration.

A second consideration that may take off the hearts of men from the things of the earth is this: the chief things that are in the earth have been the portion of reprobates heretofore and are to this day, and shall be the portion of multitudes whom God hates and has set apart to glorify His infinite justice eternally. Shall your mind and heart be set upon such things as are the portion of reprobates? Will a reprobate's portion satisfy you? Will it serve you? Are you satisfied with dog meat? If it will not content you, why is it that your mind is so much upon the things of the earth?

It may be that you are poor and low in the world. Your mind is upon some little matter. You never expect to have any great things in the world and yet you mind these little matters as if that were your portion and your happiness, some small pittance to furnish your house, to provide for yourself and your family. Oh, friend! If it were possible for you to get the empire of the whole world under your foot, still you would get no more than has been the portion of such as God has hated, and if kingdoms and empires have been the portions of reprobates, why do you abundantly mind things that are lower and let the strength of your heart flow out upon such things as these are?

A third consideration is this: surely God has made man for higher things than the things of this earth. Oh! If you had your thoughts working this way, "For what end do I think God has made the children of men? Why has He sent them into the world?" Of all the creatures God has here upon the earth, none are capable of knowing Him, the infinite First Being of all things, except the children of men. And God has given them a nature that is capable of conversing with Him. Surely, then, there are other things that God made man for, than to have meat, drink, and clothes, and to live here awhile just to enjoy creatures.

Do we not read often that Jesus Christ was God and man, took man's nature upon Himself, and died for man? Surely there must be some other manner of things that are the fruit of the purchase of the blood of Christ than the things of the earth! Oh, my brethren, if you only had this settled upon you, that God has great, glorious, high, and wonderful thoughts about mankind. This would be a mighty means to take your hearts off of the things of this earth, when you have your hearts groveling here. Oh, but are these the things God made man for? Had not God higher thoughts in making the children of men? Do not I find in the Word that when man was made there was a kind of divine consultation with the Trinity? "Come, let us make man according to our image." God had higher thoughts of man than of other things. And if man were made for nothing else but to dig in the earth, certainly, the thoughts of God about man have been very low and mean (as I may so speak with holy reverence), for these are but low and mean things here that men enjoy on the earth.

Fourth, as God has higher thoughts concerning man, so the dignity of man's nature, the rational soul of man, is of too high a birth to have the strength of it spent on things of the earth. God breathed into man His soul. It is a kind of a Divine spark. The soul of man is of the same nature as angels, a spirit as angels have. The thoughts of the mind, the faculties and powers of the soul are more precious than to be poured out as water upon the ground.

If a man had a golden mill, he would not use it just to grind dirt, straw, and sticks in. The mind of man, the thinking faculty, is too high to be exercised in the things of this earth. The mind of man is of a most excellent, capacious nature. It is fit to converse, not only with angels, but with the eternal God Himself, with Father, Son, and Holy Ghost, and to bestow the strength of such a faculty upon such dirty, drossy, low, base, mean things as earthly-minded men and women do, this is a great evil. Know this, the dignity of your nature, the excellency of your mind, and the soul of man is that of a transcendent being. Put all the world into the balance with it, it is nothing. Therefore you know what Christ said, "What shall it profit a man, to gain the whole world, and lose his soul?"

The soul of the lowest galley slave is more precious than heaven and earth, sun, moon, stars, and all the host of them and, let me add, than all the silver and golden mines under ground, and all the unsearchable riches of the great and wide sea. Yea, put all together, and the soul of the most contemptible beggar that cries for a crust of bread at your door is unexpressedly worth more than all these. Now if man's soul is of such a high-born nature, if God has put such a spirit, which is a spark of heaven, into the bosom of man for him to employ in no other use and service but to merely be an earthworm to creep upon the ground, this is a great evil.

The fifth consideration is the uncertainty of all these things, uncertain riches. Any casualty comes and takes away from you all the things of the earth that your mind is on. God sends a little too much heat into the body and puts you into a fever, and where is your delight then? Your body will either be too hot or too cold, and what's become of all your comfort in this life? You go abroad and are wounded by an enemy, and what refreshment do you receive from all these things? Let me tell you, you are in the midst of a thousand thousand casualties here, every moment ready to take away all the comforts of the earth. Usually, at the time when most minds of men and women are fixed upon the earth, that's the time God has to strike them in those things.

That's when they are closest to being deprived of the comforts of the earth, when their minds are most fixed upon them.

As you know, when the rich man in the gospel was blessing himself and crying to his soul, "Soul, soul, take thine ease. Thou hast goods laid up for many years," that very night, the text says, this message came to him, "Thou fool, this night shall thy soul be taken away from thee, and then whose shall all these things be?" And at the time that Nebuchadnezzer was blessing himself in the palace he had built for his honor, a message came to him from heaven so that he was ousted from all his court vanities to graze among the beasts of the field.

You may find in your own experience that God has many times most crossed you in the things of the earth when your minds and hearts have been most glued to them. And it may be that He has done it in mercy. It's a greater mercy to be crossed in these things at such a time than to prosper in the midst of them, for it may be a good argument that God intends good to a soul to cross him at the time he is most earthly. Oh, many who have been godly indeed, but have been earthly-minded and have found God coming at such a time and crossing them in some earthly contentment, have seen cause to bless God for thus dealing with them. "Where was I going? I was going altogether to the earth and minding such things. My heart was set upon them, and God came to me in a seasonable time to show me the vanity of my heart, and of those things that my mind was busied upon. Oh, it was a happy cross that I had at such a season! There was much of Christ that hung upon it."

Sixth, consider what has become of those who have been earthly heretofore, who enjoyed the greatest accommodations of the earth. What has become of those men in former ages of the world who lived here, and vapored so much in their generation, who had all the earth according to their desires? What's become of Agrippa and Bernice, with all their pageantry and greatness? Now they have acted their parts and are gone off the common stage of the world, and all their vanity is buried with them in one grave. What difference is there between the poor and rich when they die? They all go the same way. They lived for a little time and flourished in the things of the earth and now are gone, but have left a great deal of guiltiness behind them. Look to their example, and what's become of them? Consider that your case must be as theirs within a short while. The wheel is turning around which will bring you as low as them, so that you, before long, must be numbered among the dead. Oh, it's a mighty means to take our hearts from the things of this earth!

Seventh, consider how short the time is that you have in this world. That's the argument of the apostle, because the time is short. Therefore, let us use the world as if we used it not. Therefore, let our hearts be taken off these things. We have only a little time and a great deal of work. We have in this short winter's day of life to provide for eternity. Considering the great weight of the work that depends on us here in this world, it may be a mighty reason for us to bid adieu to all the things of this world. If we had enough time for our work, and were sure of our time, then we might spend it on trifles.

If a man comes into the city to do some business of great weight and consequence, and has only a little time to spend on it, he does not mind anything he sees in the city, he does not mind anybody that comes by him, but goes up and down the streets minding his own business. Oh, it should be so with us, brethren. Consider the great work we have to do, and the little time we have to effect that work in. Upon our little, short, uncertain inch of time, depends matters of more consequence than ten thousand, thousand worlds are worth, and if we miscarry in this little time of our lives, we are lost and undone forever.

Better we had never been born, or had been made toads or serpents, or the vilest beasts, than unreasonable creatures.

Oh, have you so much time for spending the very spirits of your souls upon the things of this earth, can you spare so many hours? Certainly, if God made known to you what eternity means, if the Lord caused the fear of eternity to fall upon you, you would not misspend as much time as you do. Many times, though, you complain of a lack of time for spiritual things. Oh, how much time do you spend in letting out your thoughts and affections upon the things of the earth? More than you need!

In the eighth place, consider that a little will carry us through this world. We are here but as on a pilgrimage or a voyage. A little will serve to carry us through this world. Men will not take more on a journey than may help them. If a man who is going on a journey should get a whole bundle of sticks and lay them on his shoulder, and you ask him the reason why he is carrying that bundle, he might say that he is going on a great journey, and he does not know how many sticks he will need to help him. Now, it's true, to carry a staff in a man's hand will help him, thus Jacob was helped by his staff over Jordan, but to carry a bundle upon his shoulder will hinder him.

A little will serve your purpose. If you have only meat and drink, food and clothing, be content, said the apostle. The servants of God in times past, passed through this world with very little, and many of them, the less they had, the more peace and comfort they had in God, and the more fit they were to die. I remember Ecolampagius was very poor when he was to die. He professed that he would not have been richer than he was, for he saw what a hindrance it was, and so he could pass out of the world with more ease and quiet. Certainly a little will serve your purpose here.

We say that nature is content with a little, and if there were grace, it would be content with less. Therefore, we do not let our minds be on the things of the earth. We do not have as much need for the things of the earth as we think we do.

Ninth, consider that there is no comfort, no good to be had in things of the earth any further than God will be pleased to let Himself through them. They are but channels to convey the blessing and goodness of God to us. Man does not live by bread or by meat only. You are deceived to think that if you had such and such things you should certainly have a comfortable life. I say you are deceived in this, for it is God in these that comforts the heart.

There is a notable Scripture for this in Psalm 62, where the Holy Ghost says in verse 10, "Trust not in oppression, and become not vain in robbery; if riches increase, set not your hearts upon them." Do not mind them, but why not? Verse 11: "God hath spoken once, twice have I heard this. That power belongeth unto God; if riches increase, set not thy heart upon them." Do not let your hearts and minds be upon riches, or anything in this earth. Why not? God has spoken again, twice have I heard, that is, again and again. God has spoken effectually to me that all power to do any good belongs to Him. It is not in riches; there is no power there to make you happy, but all belongs to Him.

This, I confess, is a spiritual meditation in which earthly-minded men will have little skill, yet where earthly-mindedness prevails in any one of the saints, this may do him good. Whereas, the truth is, this power is not in the creature, or creature comforts. Neither can do me any good. If I had a thousand times more than I have, I might be miserable in the earth and have as little comfort as those who have least. Therefore, let me set my affections upon things above, and not on things on the earth.

Tenth, lay this to heart. If you are godly, God promises to

provide the things of the earth for you, and to that end He might ease you of the burden of your care. "Cast your care upon God for He careth for you, and take no thought for these things, for your Heavenly Father knows you have need of them." Your Heavenly Father takes care; see how He clothes the lilies, and are not you much better than they? Children do not much mind the things of the earth, to provide for themselves, because they know they have their father to provide for them. A child that has his father and friends to make provision for him is very much eased by this. But those who are left fatherless and friendless seem to have some excuse, "I have to take care of myself for I have nobody to provide for me."

Aye, but the saints cannot say so; they have a Father to provide for them, and all the earth is the Lord's, as well as heaven, the earth being your Father's. The earth being the Lord's, as well as heaven, the earth being your Father's, why should your care be so much on things of the earth? Let your care be to do your duty to your Father, to walk as a child, but do not let it be for things of the earth. You as much as disavow the care of your Father for you.

Can you believe that God shall give His Son to you, and not give you all things else? Does not godliness have the promises of this life as well as of that to come? Oh, you unworthy child that professed an interest in such promises, and hoped that God had done such things for you as He has done, and yet have your heart in things of the earth. As if the Lord had settled you here only, and left you to shift for yourself from door to door. No, certainly, the care of God is over His people in the things of the earth as truly as it is over them in regard of spiritual and eternal things.

Some men think, or at least believe, that they trust God for their souls, but cannot trust Him for their bodies as well. But surely faith teaches you to trust God for your body as well as your soul, for God has care of both—and both were redeemed by the blood of Jesus Christ. I have told you that he that fears the Lord shall never want anything that is good for him. Now these considerations may mightily prevail to take off the hearts of men from the things of the earth.

The last consideration I shall name is this: all who are professors of religion are dead to the world, or should be so. Nay, if you are truly religious, you are so. By profession, you profess yourselves to be dead to the world. The Scripture makes this argument in Colossians 3:2–3: "Set your affection on things above, not on things on the earth." Why? "For you are dead, and your life is hid with Christ in God." You *are* dead, the apostle writes to the Colossians, and yet he tells them they *were* dead. The Scripture speaks much of the death of the saints. It's said of women who lived in pleasures in 1 Timothy that they were dead while they lived. So it may be said of Christians that they are dead while they live, dead to the world. "I am crucified to the world," says the apostle; and we are dead with Christ. I find that some interpret the Scripture in I Corinthians 15:29 ("Else what shall they do that are baptized for the dead?") as that all those who came in, which were heathens and converted to Christianity and were baptized, were baptized for dead men, that is, by their baptism. Now there was a profession. They professed themselves, from that time forever as dead men to the world, "baptized for the dead." You have it in some of your books "over the dead," but the word is "for," and so it is translated in this last translation, "for dead men." Your baptism is administered to you as a sign of your profession, to live henceforth as if you were dead.

This is the profession of Christians, to be as dead men to the world. Oh, do not dishonor your profession of religion; for, indeed, it is a greater evil for professors of religion to be earthly-minded than for any others, and yet how many are guilty of this? It's an observation of Luther that when God revealed Himself to Abraham and told him that He would multiply his seed, He made use of two similitudes. One was that He would make his seed as the stars of heaven; and at another time God said that He would make his seed as the sand upon the seashore. Now, said Luther, by these two expressions are signified two sorts of Abraham's seed. There are some who are as the stars of the heaven, who are heavenly-minded. There are others who are as the sand of the sea; that is, there are some who profess themselves to be of Abraham's seed, but are of earthly spirits.

Oh, now, my brethren, we should labor to have such minds and hearts so as to appear to be the seed of Abraham, as the stars of heaven, to be of the number of those who are as the stars of heaven, that is, through heavenly-mindedness. But we shall come to that when we speak of the conversation of Christians, and how it ought to be in heaven.

But now, may not someone ask, "May we not mind earthly things and heavenly things, too?" There is a great mistake here. You cannot serve two masters, God and mammon. It's very plain that the text of Scripture in Colossians 3:2 marks the opposition: "Set your affections on things above, not on things on the earth." They are opposed to one another. Set your affections or minds, for I think it is the same word as that in my text, "who mind earthly things." A man cannot look up to heaven and down to earth both at the same time. There is an opposition between these two, between the earthly-mindedness that has been opened to you and minding heavenly things.

OBJECTION. But you will say, "We have a need for these things while we are on the earth. How can we do otherwise but mind them? When we come to heaven, then we shall have dispositions suitable to heaven, and not until then."

ANSWER. Though Christians live upon the earth, they are not of the earth. There's a great deal of difference between one who is of the earth, and another who lives on the earth. Christ said concerning Himself that He was not of the earth. It's true, He did live awhile on the earth, but He was not of it. John 3:31: "He that cometh from above is above all, he that is of the earth is earthly, and speaketh of the earth." While Christ spoke these words He was on the earth, but He was not of the earth. And so it is with Christians: they are upon the earth, but they are not of the earth. They are a people redeemed from the earth!

It's true, these are things we need; therefore, we must not mind them, for in Matthew 6, where Christ speaks against taking thought for what we shall eat, or drink, or put on, He said, "Your heavenly Father knows you have need of these things." You have some need, aye, but you have need of other things, and greater need of other things than of these things. What need is there for you to live upon the earth, but in order to provide for eternity, and of living to the honor of Christ and the praise of His gospel? I say, you have no need of anything on the earth but in subordination to higher things. There is no need that you should live, except for some other end. Therefore, do not let that be an argument to plead for earthliness, as indeed an earthly spirit is very witty in pleading for itself. I shall close this point with some exhortation to you, and then give some directions about this point of earthly-mindedness.

EXHORTATIONS

Considering what has been delivered, I beseech you, lay it seriously upon your heart, especially you who are young beginners in the way of religion, lest it proves to be with you as it has with many who are digging veins of gold and silver underground. While they are digging in those mines for riches, the earth, many times, falls upon them and buries them, so that they never come up out of the mine again. And so it is with many who are beginning in the way of religion, who are digging in the mines of salvation for unsearchable riches, for that is abundantly better than gold and silver.

Now while you are thus seeking for grace and godliness, take heed that you are not covered with the earth while you are digging in the world. Keep wide open some place to heaven, or otherwise, if you dig too deep, noxious gas vapors will come up from the earth, if it doesn't fall on you first. There will be noxious gas vapors to choke you if there is not a wide hole to let in the air that comes from heaven to you. Those who are digging in mines are very careful to leave a place open for fresh air to come in. And so, though you may follow your calling and do the work that God sets you here for as others do, be as diligent in your calling as any. But still keep a passage open to heaven so that there may be fresh gales of grace come into your soul. If, at any time, you are in the world just one day, and do not have some spiritual air from heaven, take heed; there's a vapor coming up that will choke you. Oh, that Christians would consider this while they are here below!

I remember reading Augustine's comments on Psalm 72:19: "They that dwell in the wilderness shall bow before Him, and his enemies shall lick the dust." In a witty way he applied it to earthly-minded men by saying, "If you lick the dust, by this you will come to be counted as one of the enemies of God." It's true, the scope of the place is different; but take heed that, in this metaphorical sense, you do not lick the dust and so come to be counted as an enemy of God. You who would be counted as friends and seek reconciliation with God, do not lick the dust so as to always here be as moles upon the earth. Moles, though blind, are said to have their eyes open if they are on top of the ground, and then they shake and tremble. So, though the earth may close the eyes of men here for a while, certainly there will be a day when their eyes shall be opened, to see how they have guiled and deceived themselves. It's worse, too, in the time of the gospel to be an earthly-minded man than at other times. It was not such an evil thing to be an earthly-minded man in the time of the law, when all the promises of God were carried in a kind of earthly way.

This is not to say that all promises that were made under the law were merely earthly, but that they were carried out in an earthly way. Therefore you shall find that when God promised His people great mercies in the time of the law, it was done by earthly expressions, like gold, silver, and such kinds of things. Their promises for heaven went under the expression of living in the land of Canaan, as being a type of heaven. They were taken with earthly things, though, when God revealed Himself to them in an earthly manner.

Now in the time of the gospel, lift up your hearts, for your calling is from above. Now there are heavenly things revealed. He who is from above has come among us; the heavens are broken open, and the glory of it shines upon the churches in a far brighter manner than it did before. Therefore gospel light aggravates the sin of earthly-mindedness, and now, above all times, the hearts of men and women should be disengaged from the things of the earth.

CHAPTER EIGHT

$\mathcal{F}$ive $\mathcal{D}$irections $\mathcal{H}$ow to $\mathcal{G}$et our $\mathcal{H}$earts Free from $\mathcal{E}$arthly-$\mathcal{M}$indedness

1. To that end, be watchful over your thoughts. Do not take liberty to let your hearts run too far in the things of the earth. What time you have for meditation, let it be as much as can be reserved for spiritual things. Most men and women think they may take liberty in their thoughts. Why, the thing in itself is not unlawful! Aye, but your thoughts will steal upon you and affect your heart very much; therefore, watch narrowly over your thoughts, keep them within Scripture bounds.

2. Be humbled much for sin, for that will take off the heart from earthly-mindedness. Earthly-minded men, who have earthly and drossy hearts, have not known what the weight and burden of sin means. Just let God lay the weight and burden of sin upon the soul, for that will take off the soul from earthly things quickly! Oh, those men who have gone on in the world in a secure condition, and never knew what trouble of conscience meant for sin, have grown seared in those earthly contentments. But those men who have had the weight of sin lie upon them know what it is to have to deal with an infinite God. In bearing

the burden of the wrath of an incensed Deity, such men know that they have other things to look after than the things of the earth. If God would just humble your hearts, the humiliation of your spirits would quicken you, take off the dullness and deadness of your spirits, and stir you up to look after things other than the things of this life.

3. Further, set the example of the saints before you who have been the most precious servants of God in former times. Note how they counted themselves as pilgrims and strangers here on the earth. At your leisure, read Hebrews 11:13: "These all died in faith, not having received the promises, but having seen them afar off, and were persuaded of them and embraced them, and confessed that they were strangers and pilgrims on the earth."

Mark, therefore, how it follows in verse 37: "They were stoned, they were sawn asunder, were tempted, were slain with the sword, they wandered about in sheepskins and goatskins, being destitute, afflicted, tormented." Who were these people? They were those "of whom the world was not worthy. They wandered in deserts, and in mountains, and in dens and caves of the earth," and yet were such precious saints of God that the world was not worthy of them. Now when we set before us how joyfully these servants of the Most High went through all their wilderness condition, this should make us ashamed of our earthly-mindedness, and would be a mighty help to us.

4. Then, if we consider the great account that we are to give for all earthly things, you will note that you only look upon the comfort of them. But consider the account you must give for them. This would be a means to take off the heart from earthly-mindedness. And consider, what if you were now to die and go the way of all flesh. What good would it be to me to remember what contentments and pleasures I had in the earth?

5. But above all, set Jesus Christ before you and be meditating on the death of Jesus Christ. That's the great thing that will take the heart from the things of the earth. Be looking upon Christ crucified, how He who was the Lord of heaven and earth put Himself into such a low condition merely to redeem us! Conversing much with the death of Jesus Christ deadens the heart much to the world. In Philippians 3 we have a notable text for that, in the example of Paul. He counted all things as dung and dross for Jesus Christ. Verse 8: "I account all things but loss for the excellency of the knowledge of Christ Jesus my Lord, for whom I have suffered the loss of all things, and do count them but dung that I may win Christ." Then in verse 10: "That I may know Him, and the power of His resurrection, and the fellowship of His sufferings, being made conformable to His death."

Paul desired to be so conformable to the very death of Christ, that he counted all things in the world but as dung and dross in comparison of that. Paul had the death of Christ before his eyes, and meditated much on the death of Christ; and that meditation had a great impression upon his spirit. That made him count all these things as dross, as dog's meat by comparison, that he might have fellowship with the death of Christ.

Perhaps some of you think of the glory of Christ in heaven, and that may, for the present, make you less worldly. But let me entreat you to meditate on the death of Christ, and know that there is an excellency in conformity even to the death of Christ, such an excellency that may take your hearts from the things of the world. It's said of the King of France that he, asking once about an eclipse, said, "I have so much business in the earth that I take little notice of the things of heaven."

O my brethren! To close all this, I beseech you, let not this be said concerning any of you, that you have such and such worldly enjoyments that you cannot inquire about Jesus Christ. Do not plead that you have such great business, that you had so much to do in this earth, that you take little notice of the things of heaven. Surely, the saints of God have their business in heaven, as we shall, God willing, see hereafter. Their city business, their trading, their aims, their bent is higher than the things of this earth.

There are things that a man may let out his thoughts and affections to as much as he wants. This shows the vanity of the things of this world, that a man needs to be very wary how much he minds them. He cannot enjoy the comforts of this earth without some fear. But now, when he comes to converse with heaven, there he may let out himself to the uttermost. That shows the excellency of these things. You who are poor and lowly in the things of this earth, do not be discomforted because there is a charge from God that men should not mind these things. Surely there is no great matter in them since God charges that we should not mind them. Oh, the excellency lies in things above which are heavenly and spiritual, where the saints have their conversation! But of this, there is more in the following *Treatise of Heavenly Conversation.*

A Heavenly
Conversation

". . . for our conversation is in heaven. . ."

<small>PHILIPPIANS 3:20</small>

CHAPTER ONE

How Far the Examples of Godly Men Should Prevail With Us

*S*ome read the word "for" in our text as "but": "But our conversation is in heaven." Our conversation is not like theirs. Certainly the apostle intends this to make a distinction from or difference between the saints' ways and the ways of those who were enemies to the cross of Christ. "They mind earthly things, but our conversation is in heaven." But because of the word "for," I think it has reference to verse 17, for verses 18 and 19 are in a parenthesis. And therefore, if you would know the scope of the apostle in this and what this has relation to, it is in verse 17: "Brethren, be followers together of me, and mark them which walk so as you have us for an example; for our conversation is in heaven."

He made a little digression when he said, "Make us your example." Then he speaks of others who walk thus and thus, and are enemies to the cross of Christ, "whose belly is their god, whose glory is in their hands, whose end is destruction, who mind earthly things. But our [or 'for our'] conversation is in heaven." It is as if he should say, "Take heed of following those whose belly is their god, who mind earthly things, for their end is destruction; but rather follow those whose conversation is in heaven, for their end is salvation." That's the scope of the words.

From the scope and coherence of these words he is saying, "Follow us for an example, for our conversation is in heaven." So they are to be joined together. Before we speak of this heavenly conversation that the apostle mentions, we have this point: that the examples of men whose conversations are heavenly are to be followed. "Follow us, for our conversation is in heaven." They are guided by the Spirit of God and the end of their conversation is good and, therefore, 'tis safe to be followed.

In Proverbs 2:20, the wise man speaks of an argument. Why should we embrace wisdom? Because that would teach us to walk in the way of good men and to keep the paths of the righteous. It's true that the examples of the best men, though ever so holy, are not a sufficient rule for any action. If a man or woman does anything, though it is ever so good, merely upon the example of another man, yet what they do will prove to be a sin to them. I say, though the thing is good and you do it upon the example of other good men, yet if that is all the rule you have the action will be sin to you; for that is the rule of Christ to us: "Whatsoever is not of faith is sin."

Now no example can be a sufficient ground for faith. Therefore example alone is not a good rule, and sometimes we know that Satan may transform himself into an angel of light. He may, for the prevailing of some evil, make a great show of holiness. And so many gross hypocrites, for a time, have had much seeming holiness in their lives. Therefore, it must be taken for a certain truth that the examples of men, be they ever so holy, are not a sufficient rule. But thus far examples of men who are holy should prevail with us:

1. They should prevail with us more than other examples,

than examples of the most learned men. Let men be never so great Rabbis, the example of one holy man whose conversation is in heaven should be more to us than the example of many scholars. For many men who are learned may be very corrupt; they may go against their own consciences as certainly many do.

2. It should prevail against the example of great rich men who have goods laid up for many years. You should rather follow the example of those who appear to be holy than the example of the richest and greatest in the places where you live.

3. It should be more than the example of the multitude. In Joel 3:14 you have a notable Scripture against following multitudes of men. You see there that multitudes go to destruction: "Multitudes, multitudes in the valley of decision."

4. It should be more than the example of those who are merely related to us. Children should look rather at the example of godly men and women, though they are strangers, than of father or mother, uncle or aunt, or the nearest kindred. Though their examples are not rules for our faith, yet they should be more than the examples of any others.

Second, though they should not be rules or grounds of faith, yet they should be enough to take off prejudices that come from the accusations of men. If men will accuse the ways of godliness, and if there are any prejudices taken up against the paths of Zion without ground, the examples of godly men should be enough to make us stand out against them. It may be that you hear many crying out bitterly against such a way of worship; and many false aspersions are cast upon it because it is not a national way of worship, for few follow it. Do but observe what manner of persons worship God in the way that some call heresy. Are they not of a holy and blameless conversation according to the gospel, the strictest Puritans? Now though you must not do as they do merely from their example, yet their example should have a great deal of power and influence upon you to take off prejudices, answer accusations, and calm and sweeten your angry and bitter spirits.

Third, examples, though not sufficient ground and rule for faith, should be enough to make us inquire after those ways, to examine and try whether they have any footing in the Word, because the followers of them are very upright and circumspect in their ways. Let me at least inquire after these ways; let me examine them by the light of the gospel. Surely there is some probability that these ways are the very paths of Zion and lead to the gate of heaven, because the professors of them are such friends of Jesus Christ. It's likely that these men should know the mind of God who converse with God the most, who lie in His bosom as the beloved disciple did in Christ's.

Is it not more likely that a man who is a familiar friend and converses daily with a man should know his secrets, his will, more than a stranger? So all men in the world are strangers to God except the saints. They converse with God; they are the men of His counsel and His heart. Therefore, of all the men in the world, it's most likely that they should have all the will of God revealed unto them. All learning and natural wisdom cannot show the mind of God as much as conversing with God and a holy, humble familiarity with Him. God loves to open His bosom to His hidden ones, to reveal His mind to them; and therefore, when we see men who are godly, whose conversation is in heaven, it should make us think it likely that there is more good in these ways than I am presently aware of.

It's likely that God smiles upon such men, that they should know the mind of God more than other men. Therefore, though I will not yet conclude it is the mind of God and do something merely because they do it, at least I will examine and search whether or not it is the mind of God according to the Scriptures.

Fourth, the example of godly men should prevail far enough to make us take heed that we do not oppose those ways unless we have clear ground to the contrary. Then we may oppose them as Paul opposed Peter and resisted him to his face, because he did not go in the right way. Let men be ever so holy and godly, they may still be opposed in their way. If, upon examination, you see clearly that this is not the way of God, and you find it to be otherwise (not because others think so, or because so and so are contrary to it, no, but because you have been examining the situation by the Word of God, and laying the rule to your conscience, consequently you find it to be disagreeable to the mind of God), then you may speak or write against it, but do not do it otherwise.

If you see men who are holy, men whose conversations are in heaven, don't oppose them because other men do. Be sure your ground is good, and you are clear in it if you do oppose it; otherwise you may be in danger of fighting against God when you oppose them. Therefore, make so much use of the example of godly, holy men as not to oppose the way except upon clear Scripture evidence to the contrary.

Fifth, the example of godly men should prevail with us to prepare us to let in any truth that they do profess and practice. When we examine what the ways of God and heaven are, let us come with prepared hearts to let in the truths God shall reveal unto us, and all the more because we see such holy and godly men have embraced those truths before us. When precious gospel truths are delivered to us by the hands of the servants of Jesus Christ, then those very truths are like apples of gold in pictures of silver, as beautiful as golden fruit in silver dishes.

Sixth, the example of godly men should prevail with us so

that after we have examined and found their way to be according to the truth indeed, then their example should confirm us in the truth, should help to settle us more in the truth, should comfort and encourage us in such and such holy courses. We find not only that we are convinced of it, and we see it to be the way of God and have experience of it, but others see it and they are convinced of it. Others who are so godly find much communion with God in it.

Now this should mightily strengthen and further us since we are going the same way that the saints of God have gone in. Indeed, it should be a great grief to any godly man that he should differ from other godly men. Although, we cannot help being different from other godly men because we are imperfect here, and sometimes a weak Christian knows that of which a strong Christian may be ignorant. It turns out sometimes that God, in some things, reveals Himself to those who are weak and hides Himself from those that are strong; so here in the world it cannot be expected to be otherwise for the present, until that time when the New Jerusalem shall be let down from God out of heaven, and then the saints will be all of one mind and walk all in one way. But until then, it should be expected that saints will have different ways. But yet I say, it should be a very great heart-trouble to godly men to see that they are forced to go in different ways from other godly men. And, on the other side, it should be a great encouragement and strengthening when the saints go on in one way together with their faces towards heaven.

CHAPTER TWO

What's to Be Done When Examples of Godly Men Are Contrary?

f you say, "What should we do when we have contrary examples and both sides are godly men, yea, very godly men, whose conversation is in heaven? Some go one way and others, as godly as they, go another way. What shall people do, then, when they see that holy men go either way?" To that I answer only these two things:

First, God, by this means, puts you to a stricter examination of things and teaches you by this that every Christian, though ever so weak, should have a bottom and ground for their faith, and practice the Word for themselves. Never did God teach this lesson more strongly than He is doing now. None of us should satisfy ourselves in any point of religion, nor in any practice of religion, other than what we can find footing for out of the Word.

In former times Christians were very much led by examples, and a few exemplary godly professors would carry all the well-affected in those places with them. All who pretended godliness would be very loath to go in a different way from some eminent, godly men. But though their affections might be good, and God might accept their good affections, they certainly were not as grounded and established in the truth as God would have them. But now the Lord seems to go another way with His people, and puts each one, the weakest, the lowest servant, to searching and finding the truth for themselves, and to have the knowledge of it for themselves. We hope the time is at hand for the fulfilling of that promise that all the people shall be taught of God, shall be taught to understand what are the reasons and grounds of the practice of religion, of those tenets and opinions which they hold. And when people come to understand the grounds themselves they have a great deal more strength, and they will come to be established more than they formerly were.

Second, when you see examples on both sides going contrary one to the other, and both are godly, examine this: which way has the most earthly inducements? For that way lies under the most suspicion that has more earthly inducements to draw or bias the heart. Men who are godly are but godly in part; and though they may be as godly as other men in some things, yet there may be a temptation. If the temptation for earthly contentment lies more in one way than the other, you are to be more wary of one way than the other.

Rebuke of Those Who Follow the Example of the Wicked and Reject the Example of the Godly

*I*f the example of men whose conversation is in heaven is to be followed, it follows then that they are to be rebuked who follow the example of wicked or ungodly ones. If these wicked or ungodly ones are great or learned, the multitude will follow the example of anyone except those whose conversation is in heaven. You do thus and so and excuse it by saying, "Do not others do so?" But who are these people who do so? Can you say in your conscience that you think these people have their conversations in heaven and that is why you do as you do? If there is any example you should follow, it should be such as you can take upon your consciences that these are the men who have their conversations above.

You do as others do in drinking, swearing, Sabbath-breaking, and in all manner of profaneness. Do these have their conversation in heaven? Certainly you who do so follow the example of those who have their conversations in hell. But it may be you have some neighbors whose conversations are blameless, yea, they are heavenly. And when you are in a good mood, your consciences witness to them and you wish that you might die the death of the righteous. Are there not some who live in the same families, streets, or towns where you live who, though sometimes your hearts are against them, and you oppose them, and scorn them, and speak against them, yet when you are in any good temper, or are afraid of death, then you wish you were as they are and might die their death. Now, will you not follow their example rather than the example of others whose examples are in such things as are suitable to your vile, sinful, base lusts?

We know that these examples of holy men shall rise up in judgment against you another day. The Lord will condemn you by their example and say, "Did not such and such live in the family and place where you lived? And did you not behold their holy and gracious conversation? And shall the example of such and such vile wretches be followed rather than the example of My saints?" I say, this will stop your mouths and aggravate your condemnation in the great Audit Day.

There are some who are so far from following the example of those whose conversation is in heaven that they rage and fret against them, and do what they can to darken the glory of their holy lives. If they can find any bad report about them they will follow it to the end so that they can eclipse the holiness of their lives in order to quiet their own consciences. Whereas, were there not something to darken the luster and beauty of the lives of the saints, men's hearts would surely condemn them for walking in ways contrary to them. Therefore, for the relief of their consciences, that they might not condemn them for walking in ways contrary to them, they do what they can to spit upon their glory. They are glad if they can hear any bad report of them and they will follow it to the uttermost, and all because their corrupt hearts are against the holiness of their lives and conversations.

Last, let those who profess religion labor to walk so that their examples may be convincing others. Is there such a power in holy examples to prevail with men? You who profess religion, make this an argument to work upon your hearts so that your conversation may be more in heaven, so your example may do more good in the place where you live. You who profess religion and yet have earthly spirits and live scandalously, know that you do almost as much mischief as a man can do in this world. There is no greater mischief than for one to profess religion and yet have his conversation be wicked and ungodly and, by this, to lie about his profession.

CHAPTER FOUR

Two Doctrines Observed From the Text

hus we proceed to the principal doctrinal truths, "for our conversation is in heaven," that is, our city conversation, our citizen-like behavior, our city estate; for the word signifies our carriage, our conduct. Like free denizens, it is in heaven. Now, from this, you have these two doctrines:

1. The saints are the citizens of heaven.
2. Their behavior, their conversation, even while they are in this world, is in heaven.

1. For the first (just briefly to make way for the second), the saints of God are the citizens of heaven. They are all free denizens, burgesses of heaven. In Ephesians 2:19, you may see how God has gathered all the saints together to be fellow citizens of heaven: "Now therefore ye are no more strangers and foreigners, but fellow citizens with the saints and of the household of God." They have a heavenly city here in the church. The church is a heaven to the saints, and a type of that heaven where they shall come to live forever, both with the saints and

angels hereafter. In Hebrews 11:9-10, it's spoken of Abraham, "He sojourned in the land of promise, as in a strange country, dwelling in tabernacles with Isaac and Jacob, the heirs with him of the same promise, for he looked for a city which hath foundations, whose builder and maker is God."

It seems, then, that all the cities in the world, in comparison to this city, have no foundations. Abraham looked for a city that has foundations and whose builder and maker is God. The builders and makers of these cities are men. The founders of the most famous cities in the world have been men, and many times wicked and ungodly men. The first city that we read of was built by Cain. The builders and makers of these cities are men, laboring men, but Abraham looked for a city whose builder and maker is God. Hebrews 12:22: "But ye are come unto Mount Zion, and unto the city of the living God, the heavenly Jerusalem." Mark it, "and to an innumerable company of angels," so that you are then to have them for your fellow citizens. The saints of God here in the church are said to dwell in heaven, but in their city there are an innumerable company of angels also. That plainly notes that it has reference to the glorious heaven of which the saints are citizens.

The saints are citizens of heaven; it is there that they dwell. Revelation 13:6-7: "And he opened his mouth in blasphemy against God, to blaspheme His name and His tabernacle, and them that dwell in heaven. And it was given unto him to make war with the saints, and to overcome them." Now these were not in heaven, but they are said to dwell in heaven because they are of the church here. And they are free denizens of heaven, too, of the heaven of the saints where they shall live in a more glorious way. They are citizens of it now, and they may be said to dwell in heaven, as we shall see afterwards in the opening of their conversations being in heaven.

CHAPTER FIVE

How the Saints Are Citizens of Heaven

1. First, the saints are citizens of heaven for their names are all enrolled in heaven. They are written in heaven, as in Luke 10:20: "Rejoice in this, that your names are written in heaven." In heaven is the Book of Life, where all the names of the saints are written. Philippians 4:3: "whose names are written in the book of life."

2. The saints are citizens of heaven for they have Christ their Head gone before to take possession of heaven in their names. Therefore they have a right to heaven in the same way that a man who is a citizen of one country remains a citizen even while he travels through a strange country. He is said to be a citizen still, even though he is bodily in a strange land for the present. So the saints have their names enrolled in heaven. Jesus Christ their Head has gone before them in their names, to take possession for them and to provide mansions for them, as in John 14.

3. When they actually believe, they take up their freedom. Their names were enrolled from all eternity. And so Christ, at His ascension, went and took possession. But when they actually believe, they take up their freedom in Christ. There are

many men who are born free, yet there is a time when they take it up. And so others, who have served for their freedom, may wait a long time before they are actually made free. When the saints actually come to believe, they take up their freedom in the city of heaven and are made free burgesses of heaven.

4. In the fourth place, they are no longer slaves. They are not bond-slaves like before; they are delivered from bondage, being made free for heaven. When foreigners or slaves become citizens they have the same freedoms that others have.

They are admitted to city privileges and are no longer seen as slaves. So when those who are by nature bond-slaves to sin and Satan, such as are under the bondage of the law, come to believe, they are enfranchised in heaven and are delivered from the bondage of the law, sin, and Satan. They are said to be free men of the city of heaven.

5. All the saints have right to all the common stock, treasury, and riches of heaven. Whatever privileges belong to the charter of heaven, the saints have right and title to them all. In great cities there is a common stock and treasury that is for public occasions, and every citizen has some interest in it. So the saints have interest in all the common stock and treasury, and all the riches that there are in heaven.

6. The saints are the citizens of heaven. They have, for the present, the same confirmation of their happy estate that the angels and those blessed souls have who are residents of heaven. They have this privilege now by being citizens of heaven. Though their bodies are not in the highest heavens, yet they have their happiness confirmed as surely as do the angels and any blessed souls in Abraham's bosom. Look how they are confirmed in a happy estate, so that they cannot be made miserable. So it is with every believer. Though he lives in this world, he has the privilege of being a citizen of heaven. He is

confirmed in a happy estate; all the powers of hell and in the world can never make this soul to be miserable. This is a mighty privilege of being a citizen of heaven. He is more privileged than Adam was in paradise, for Adam was not confirmed and established when he was made in the state of innocence. But every believer is as confirmed and established as the angels in heaven.

7. They have this privilege: by being citizens they have privilege of free trade to heaven. You know that freemen in the city have privilege of trade more so than foreigners. Foreigners are made to pay more customs and taxes than free citizens. So the saints have the privilege of free trade in heaven for anything that concerns them; they have a free course in heaven that others do not have.

8. They now have communion with the angels of heaven. There is communion and commerce between the saints here and the angels upon this ground, because they are fellow citizens. In the passage in Hebrews that we quoted earlier, "We are come to the heavenly Jerusalem, and to the innumerable company of angels," there is a great deal of intercourse between the saints and angels here upon the earth. The angels look upon them as their fellow citizens, and are ministering spirits for the good of the elect. They do great services for the churchmen here in this world for this reason: they look upon them as their fellow citizens.

9. They have the protection of heaven, being the citizens of heaven. They have heaven's protection. One who is a citizen has the protection of the law of the city and the power of the city to defend him. Hence we read that it was dangerous to meddle with Paul because he was a Roman. In Acts 22:25, as they bound him with thongs, Paul said unto the centurion standing by, "Is it lawful for you to scourge a man that is a Roman, and uncon-

demned?" It was as if he should say, "Take heed of what you do. I am free of the city of Rome." Mark it, when the centurion heard that, he went and told the chief captain, saying, "Take heed what you do, for this man is a Roman; he has the protection of the city."

Thus the saints are citizens of heaven; they are not Romans, but of the heavenly Jerusalem. And when any are about to wrong one of them, they need to take heed of what they do, for he is a citizen of heaven. The King of heaven is his King to protect him, and He sits and laughs at the enemies of the church. The very angels themselves are their guard, to guard all these citizens and to protect them. This is the comfortable estate of all the people of God, that they are the citizens of heaven. All this I note out of the meaning of the words in the original. And without the understanding of the propriety of the language and the words, we would not have the understanding of this truth.

This being so, it should teach all the people of God to walk as is becoming citizens, and not to be rude in their behavior. 'Tis a dishonor for citizens to be rude in their behavior. It is enough for country people who never had any education to be rude, but the saints of God have the education of heaven (this could even be added as a tenth particular). They have the Holy Ghost to be their Instructor, to bring them up in holy and good manners suitable to heaven. This the saints have. Manifest it in your conversation; do not be rude in your way. Prize the privilege of being a citizen of heaven. It's that which cost Jesus Christ dearly to purchase this enfranchisement and liberty for you.

We read in Acts 22 of the captain who heard that Paul was a Roman. In verse 27, the chief captain said to him, "Tell me, art thou a Roman?" Paul said, "Yes." Then the chief captain answered, "With a great sum I obtained this freedom." To which Paul answered, "I was free born." They used to give great sums to purchase freedoms of the city. Oh, the city that we are speaking of has privileges beyond any in the world! And no man or woman can come to be free of this city but by a great purchase. No man can say as Paul did that he was free born. If he came to be free with regard to heaven, it was with a great purchase. It was with the purchase of the blood of Jesus Christ, which was worth more than all the world.

"If the Son shall make you free, then you shall be free indeed." Therefore, prize this as a great mercy. While you live here in this world, account it as a great mercy that you are a citizen of heaven. Account your happiness to consist there; it is more than to have houses and lands here. For a man to have a freedom of some city is more than to have house and land in the wilderness. Though the Lord orders things so that while you live in the wilderness of this world you have no habitation of your own, yet certainly the Lord has made you free of heaven. It was purchased by the blood of Jesus Christ for you. By the price that it cost, you may conclude that there is some great matter in it, that you are a free denizen of heaven.

CHAPTER SIX

How the Saints Have Their Conversation in Heaven

*T*he conversation of the saints who are free citizens of heaven ought to be suitable. Though their cohabitations is in this world, their conversation should be in heaven. In Daniel 7:18, you read of the excellent estate of the saints: "But the saints of the Most High shall take the kingdom, and possess the kingdom forever." That part which is translated "the saints of the Most High" does not only mean of the Most High God, but the saints of the high places. That is how some translated it, for the saints are the saints of high places in regard of their interest in heaven, and in regard of their conversations being suitable to that place. Ephesians 2:6: "And hath raised us up together, and made us fit together in heavenly places in Christ Jesus." The saints are set in heavenly places, and are given heavenly dignity, heavenly privileges, and heavenly prerogatives; yea, and they themselves may be said to be in heavenly places though their bodies are upon the earth. Their souls are in heavenly places; their conversation is in heaven. They are the saints of the high God and they are set in high places.

You might ask, "What is this conversation in heaven that is spoken of here?" I shall open it here in these particulars:

1. The aim and scope of their hearts is heavenward. That which the saints look at as their aim and scope is heaven. They look upon themselves in this world as pilgrims and strangers. Heaven is their home and their eye is there. Their end, their scope, whatever they do is for heaven, to one way or another fit them for heaven. They shall come and live there; therefore their conversation is in heaven. In all that they do—eating, drinking, going about their business—their aim is heaven.

It's reported that Anaxagorus, a philosopher, being asked where he lived, said that he was born to contemplate the heavens. He made it the end of his life; he was born to contemplate the heavens. Being a philosopher, and having understanding of the motions of the heavens, he took such a delight in them that he counted it the end for which he was born. So the saints look at heaven as the center at which they aim; that's their scope. The apostle said that we do not look at things that are seen, but at things that are not seen. Nothing in the earth is our scope; heaven is our scope. So the saints' conversations may be said to be in heaven in that respect.

2. Their conversations are in heaven for they act on heavenly principles in all their ways. "Heavenly principles," you will say, "what are they?" This is a heavenly principle: God is all in all. That's a principle that the saints are guided by. In heaven, they look upon God to be all in all unto them. So do the saints here. In what they do, in what they are, in what they enjoy, they act upon this principle: God is all in all. Whatever I see in the creature, it is God who is all in all to me. I act by virtue of this principle.

It is a heavenly principle that God, the infinite First Being, is infinitely worthy of all love for Himself. The saints in heaven look upon the infinite excellency and glory of God; they look upon Him as the First Being of all things, having all excellency and glory enough to satisfy all creatures forever. They look upon Him as infinitely worthy of all love and service for Himself. Know that this is a heavenly principle. So because the saints' conversation is in heaven, they act on heavenly principles.

It is an earthly principle that I look upon such and such things in the world whereby I may go in credit, increase, or comfort. But when my heart is so upon God that it looks on Him as infinitely excellent and worthy of all love, service, fear, honor, and worship for Himself alone whatever becomes of the creature, God is worthy of all, because of that infinite excellency in Himself—this is a heavenly principle. And for one to act in his life by a principle such as this is to act according to heavenly principles, not by such low and base principles as the men of the world, but by heavenly principles.

3. Their conversations are in heaven. Though they live in the world, they have communion with the God of heaven above in the whole course of their lives. In I John 1, you have divers excellent expressions about our communion with God. Verse 3: "That which we have seen and heard declare we unto you, that ye also may have fellowship with us, and truly, our fellowship is with the Father and with His Son, Jesus Christ." And then, in another Scripture, we read of the communion of the Holy Ghost. There is communion with the Father, Son, and Holy Ghost. Now what makes heaven to be heaven but God? We say that where the king is, there is the court. Where God is there is heaven, let God be where He will.

There is some controversy among some as to where the saints shall be after the resurrection. Some think it shall be here still, with all the glory that the Scripture speaks of. It is no great matter where it is, just so it is where God is. Those who have communion with God are in heaven; they have their conversation in heaven. It is that which is the life of the saints, their communion with God. Your life is to have communion with the creature, that is, for you to close with the contents of the creature. The faculty that is in any man to taste anything, or to have any delight in anything in this world, when there is an object suitable to that faculty, that is communion with the creature. For example, a drunkard has a kind of communion with his lewd company, to please his senses for a while. That's all the communion he has. But what a different conversation is this, for one merely to please his senses with meat or drink for a little while, and another to have communion with the Father, Son, and Holy Ghost! The saints in this world do not have an imaginary, but a real communion with the Father, Son, and Holy Ghost.

"Communion," you will say, "what's that?" By communion with God we mean the acting of the soul upon God, and receiving the influence of the goodness, love, and mercy of God into the soul. When there is a mutual acting of the soul upon God and God upon the soul, there is a mutual embracing and opening of hearts one to the other for the satisfying of one another's spirits. It is as when friends have communion with one another, that is, when one acts for the comfort of the other. So communion with God is the mutual acting of the soul upon God, and God upon the soul in return. The saints see the face of God, and God delights in the face of the saints. They let out their hearts to God, and God lets out His heart to them.

We cannot express this to strangers. A stranger cannot understand this joy. This is a mystery, a riddle to the carnal world. Consider that whatever communion you have with your lewd company, sitting, eating, drinking, playing, and telling stories all day long, you think constitutes a splendid life. The communion of the saints is raised to a higher level, and the comfort of the saints is not in such poor, low, base things as yours is. The saints have comfort in God the Father, Son, and Holy Ghost in an infinitely higher way, and, in that respect, their conversations are said to be in heaven. They are unable to be content when they are with God in His ordinances unless they have communion with God there in a special way. It is not enough for them to call upon the name of God, to kneel down and use some humble, broken-hearted expressions. "Oh, what communion do I have with God, and Jesus Christ, and the Holy Ghost in my duties at this time? I come to the Word and other ordinances, but what communion do I have with God in them? I cannot be satisfied unless I can taste and see how good the Lord is. I cannot go abroad and be about my business with anything but a heavy heart unless I hear something from heaven this morning." All the comfort of their lives depends upon having communion with Father, Son, and Holy Ghost.

4. Their conversation may be said to be in heaven because they live according to the laws of heaven. They do not live in this world according to the laws of men and the lusts of men, but they look to heaven for their direction. "What rule is there from heaven to guide me?" There must be some word from the God of heaven to order and guide them in their ways or else they cannot tell what is suitable for them. Indeed, while they live in the cities of the world they must obey the laws of men, but still it is in order to the laws of heaven. The main thing to which they submit is the statute laws of Jesus Christ, the great Lawgiver.

Because there is a law of heaven that requires them to obey the laws of men that are according to the laws of heaven, they obey them. But the laws of heaven are those that the saints look to for their direction in all their ways. "Such and such a thing I have a mind to, but will the law of heaven justify me in this? Have I any word from Jesus Christ to guide me in such a way? I dare not do otherwise than according to the will and scepter of Christ; they must be my rule in all my ways." Before your lust and your own ends were your rule; the common course of the world was your rule, not the laws of heaven. And therefore their conversations are in heaven because they are guided by the laws of heaven. Heaven is their aim; they act upon heavenly principles; they converse with the God of heaven, and they live according to the laws of heaven.

5. Their thoughts and hearts are set upon heaven. As the saying goes, "The soul is where it loves rather than where it lives." Where the heart is, there's the soul, and there the man may be said to be. Now the saints have their hearts in heaven; their thoughts in heaven, their meditations in heaven. "When I am awake I am always with Thee," said David. And, oh, how sweet are the thoughts of heaven unto the saints! While you are wallowing in the world, plodding for yourself in the things of this world, God might come to you and ask, "Where are you?" as He did to Adam. While you are in prayer or hearing the Word, where are your thoughts, and what are they about?

One whose conversation is in heaven keeps his thoughts and meditations there continually, meditating on the glorious things that are reserved in heaven. I remember reading of that holy man, Mr. Samuel Ward, who, in the midst of a dinner, broke out crying, "Forever, forever, forever," for about 7 or 8 minutes. He could not be quieted, but kept crying, "Forever, forever, forever." As far as any man has his conversation in heaven, his thoughts are there, thinking, "Oh, eternity, eternity, to be forever in heaven, to live forever with Christ and God, and, oh, the crown of glory that is there! When will that blessed day come when I shall come to enjoy those good things that are there?" His thoughts will be there and he is longing to be there; his love, desires, and affections will be working there.

It's said of the people of Israel in Acts 7:39 that their hearts turned back again to Egypt. They never returned in their bodies to Egypt, but their hearts were there. They would happily have had the onions and the fleshpots of Egypt. Their hearts were there. So it may be said of many that, though they come and hear the Word, their hearts are still in their shops; their hearts are after their covetousness. But it's not so with the saints. Though they live here in this world, their hearts are in heaven.

I remember it was written of Queen Mary that she said that if they ripped her open they would find tea in her heart. And so it may be said of saints whose conversation is in heaven, who walk with God and live lives of heaven here upon earth: if they were ripped open, you would find heaven in their hearts. I do not speak of all professors of religion, for when Paul speaks of the resurrection he speaks of celestial bodies and terrestrial bodies. So I say there are celestial professors and terrestrial professors. If you ripped open many men's hearts there would be nothing but the earth, uncleanness and baseness. Suppose God were to come this moment and rip up all your hearts, revealing them to all the men of the world, what filthy stuff would be found in many of your hearts? But for those whose conversations are in heaven, they would be ready to have God rip open their hearts whenever He pleases. "Lord, Lord, try me, search me, examine and see what is in my heart!"

I'll put this to you now in the name of God, and let your conscience answer. What do you think would be found in your hearts if they should be ripped open now? If your consciences tell you, "O Lord, if my heart should be ripped up now, there would be a filthy deal of ugly and abominable stuff there. Surely I have not had my conversation in heaven; my heart has been sinking down to low and base things." But for those whom this text concerns, it will be a great comfort to them. I hope there are several of you who may be able to say, "If the Lord should rip our hearts and show them to all the world, I hope the world would see that heaven is stamped on our hearts."

We count it sad weather when we cannot see the heavens for many days, when we cannot see heaven, many times, for a week. We consider it a bad home where men dwell in narrow lanes in the city, so that they can scarcely see the heavens unless they go into the fields. My brethren, surely it's a sad time with a gracious heart when one day passes without conversing with heaven, without the sight of heaven, without meditations of heaven, without having their hearts there.

Thus it should be with Christians whose conversations are in heaven. They should never love such dwellings wherein they cannot see the beams of the sun. It's a most comfortable thing to see the light. To a man who dwells in some dark house, it's very comforting to walk out into the open air and behold the heavens. O my brethren! Our souls dwell in dark houses, every one of us, for our bodies are to our souls like a dark and low cellar; but the Lord gives us liberty to go abroad, to be conversing with the things of heaven that He has revealed in His Word and in His ordinances.

Many citizens who live in dark rooms and work long hours, on days of recreation take long walks in the fields and smell the fresh air. How delightful it is to them! The same should be true of a gracious heart, even though he has much business in the world. On the Lord's Day he may enjoy God in His ordinances more than before. His thoughts are on those ways where he may come to have more of heaven! "Oh, that I may come to converse more with God than at other times." And upon that, the Sabbaths are the joy of his soul, his delight. He longs after the Sabbaths; he thirsts after ordinances, for indeed his heart is in them, for he finds there is more of heaven in them than in other things. In that regard, the saints, having their thoughts and hearts in heaven, prove their conversation to be in heaven.

Moses never came to Canaan, and yet God gave Moses a sight of it and carried him up to Mount Nebo. Heavenly meditations are, as it were, Mount Nebo whereby, when the heart is raised a little upon the mount it is able to see heaven and behold the glorious things there. The Scripture speaks of Lucifer having had his nest among the stars. A saint has, as it were, his nest, his dwelling among the stars, yea, above the stars in the highest heavens. Wicked men seem to draw nigh to God, yet their hearts are far from Him; their hearts are still in their shops. They are in their shops or ships when they seem to be worshipping God. Though the saints are far from God bodily, yet their hearts are in heaven in the meantime.

6. A heavenly conversation consists of this: when in the course of men's lives they converse and delight in the same things that are done in heaven. They make their happiness the same happiness that is in heaven, and make their exercise to be the same exercise that is in heaven. For instance, what is there in heaven? There is the sight of the face of God, "Blessed are the pure in heart, for they shall see God." And the angels always behold the face of God. So the saints may be said to have their conversations in heaven because their exercise here, while they live, is beholding the face of God, in standing before God, and seeing His face. The greatest delight and contentment of their souls is that they can see something of God.

What's to be done further? The work of heaven is praising and blessing God. What do the saints and angels of heaven do but continually bless, magnify, and praise the name of that God whom they see to be so infinitely worthy of all praise and honor from His creatures? Then is a man's conversation in heaven when, in doing the same things, he joins the angels and saints in doing the same work, magnifying and blessing and praising God.

What's done in heaven but keeping a perpetual Sabbath? Then are our conversations in heaven when we delight in God's Sabbath, and keep a constant Sabbath unto God, though we are busy with earthly things. We can still keep a Sabbath to God by resting from sin and being spiritually employed.

7. Our conversation is in heaven when in earthly employments we are heavenly, when we use earthly things after a heavenly manner. It is not the place where God's saints are that He looks at as much as what they do. Though we use earthly things while we live on the earth, when we use them in a heavenly manner, then our conversation is in heaven though we are on the earth.

In the use of earthly things we quickly pass from earthly things to God. We make use of them but we do not stick to them. We make them the means to pass on to God, and we go quickly. A carnal heart sticks to the things of the earth and mingles with the earth; but a spiritual, heavenly heart makes earthly things just conduits to convey him to heaven. We carry with us our flesh, and because we have so much earth, we have need of these earthly things; but they are means of conveying on to spiritual and heavenly things.

We use earthly things as heavenly, that is, we use earthly things to meditate on heaven. Enjoying anything in this earth raises our thoughts to things of heaven. When we see the light we remember the glorious light of heaven and the inheritance of the saints who are in light. We see some sweetness in the creature, and if these things are so sweet, oh, what is heaven and God then, who is the Fountain of all good things! Thus, to make all earthly things to be heavenly things, that's a heavenly conversation. Using earthly things to make us think of God, that's a heavenly conversation.

8. Our conversation is heavenly when the saints in their conversation together are heavenly, when the saints in their conversations look upon themselves as the citizens of heaven and converse as becomes those of such a country. When men go abroad to foreign lands and meet together, and confer about the state of their country in their own language, about friends and such things, they often will say to one another, "I feel like I am in England now; our conversation is as if I was in England." So when the saints meet, they do not meet to jangle and wrangle, but they meet to converse about heaven. There are no saints who walk closely with God who do not tell each other about some tidings of salvation when they meet together. When Englishmen meet together in any place, the first question is usually, "What news is there from England?" So when saints meet together, if they are of heavenly conversation, they will be talking of heaven before they go. What news do you have of our country? What news of heaven? Though they may have liberty to refresh themselves, being poor earthly creatures, with something of the earth, yet they will have some talk of heaven before they part company. This is a heavenly conversation, when the communion of the saints of heaven is about heavenly things.

9. The last thing wherein the conversation of the saints in heaven consists is this: their great trade while they are upon the earth is for heaven. Though they are not there bodily, their trading is there; and that's the special thing that seems to be

noted in the very word in the text. The saints who have heavenly conversations do not trade for trifles as other men do; they trade for great things, for high things. In Colossians 3, Paul says, "If ye be risen with Christ, seek those things that are above where Christ sitteth at the right hand of God; set your affections on things above and not on things of the earth." They seek the things of God, those things where Christ sits at the right hand of God. Set your affections on things above and not on things on the earth. They seek after these things; they merchandise for those goodly pearls.

CHAPTER SEVEN

The Saints' Trading for Heaven

There are several things to be considered in the saints' trading for heaven. First, in trade it is required that those who are tradesmen to any country have skill in the commodity for which they trade. So the saints have skill in heavenly things. There are many poor Christians who have little skill in the matters of the world. Speak to them about worldly things and they understand only a little, but speak to them about heaven and you may quickly perceive that they have skill in heavenly commodities. They have a skill from God; they are wise merchants.

Second, a tradesman must have a stock to trade with. The saints have a stock to trade with for heaven; they have grace in their hearts. Grace in the heart is a stock for a trade. If you leave your children no lands, but leave them a good trade and a stock, you will think you have left them a plentiful portion.

Now the saints, though they have just a little in the world, have skill in the commodities of heaven. They have a good trade and a good stock too. They have a stock of grace that shall never be lost. They may not have the income that they desire sometimes, yet they shall never lose their stock, their portion, and they should be careful to improve their stock for heaven. They have their conversation in heaven then when they improve and lay out all their stock that way about heavenly commodities.

A third thing in trading is to take advantage of the market for commodities. Great bargains may be had sometimes that cannot be had at another. So the trade of a Christian for heaven is in observing the advantages he has for heavenly things. Those who have their conversation in heaven are very wise and understanding in this way. They are able to know their times and seasons. Other men who do not have skill in the matters of heaven do not know their times and seasons, therefore they neglect their markets. Perhaps on their sick and deathbed they begin to think of heaven, and then, oh, that they might know that their soul was going to heaven when they leave their bodies! But you are unskilled in heavenly commodities. You did not know your time; you should have had your conversation in heaven in the time of your life, and then you would have observed what advantages God gave you for trading for heaven.

Oh, that we were all wise this way, to make it appear that our conversations are in heaven in this respect, that we are wise to observe our advantages. Oh, the advantages God has given us all at one time or another for heaven! There's not any one of you to whom God has not given much advantage for heaven had you just taken it. If you will reflect upon your own hearts, the course of your lives in former times, your consciences may tell you, "Oh, sometimes what fair advantages I had for heaven! How the Spirit of God began to stir in me. What truths were darted into me at such a season. What motions I had flowing in. Oh, how happy I would have been had I taken such advantages for heaven. I would have been in heaven already!"

Now those who converse with heaven watch for those

advantages. They do not come to hear the Word, but they watch for the time to have God stirring in their hearts. They follow that advantage; they watch for the time of the softening of their spirits and the enlivening of their souls. They follow those advantages hard, and so trade for heaven and grow rich in heavenly commodities.

Fourth, where there is trade from one country to another, there's much intercourse. A man who trades to such a town or country has much intercourse between himself and those who live there. A Christian's trading for heaven is this: there is much intercourse between heaven and his soul. Every day he sends up to heaven, and every day he has something from heaven sent down to his soul!

Oh, examine what intercourse there has been between heaven and you! How is it with many of you? Is it as if there is no heaven at all? Men who do not trade with the Indies act as if there were no such place at all. So it is with many who live in the bosom of the church. There is very little intercourse between heaven and them. But a trader for heaven has much intercourse with heaven.

Fifth, a man who trades great amounts has the chief of his stock where he trades. Though he is not present in his body, yet the chief of his estate is there. If a man is a Spanish or Turkish merchant and trades there, the chief of his estate lies in Spain or Turkey more than here. So it is with one who trades for heaven: the chief part of his estate lies there. He accounts his riches to lie in heaven. Indeed, he has something to live on here in this world for a while, but his riches are there. He looks at heaven as the place where his greatest treasure lies.

Sixth, a man who trades is willing to part with something where he is so that he may receive an advantage in the place where he trades. So it is with the saints who trade for heaven:

they are willing to part with much here so that they might receive something afterwards in heaven. They are willing to part with anything here in this world to the end that they may receive it when they come home. A carnal heart that does not know the certainty or excellency of the commodities of heaven is willing to part with nothing, but will keep all. That heart thinks to itself, "What I have here I am sure of, but that which is said of heaven, I do not know what it is. It may prove to be just an imaginary thing; therefore I will keep what I have and be sure of that." Oh, you are no trader for heaven. If you were, you would be willing to part with anything here that you might receive commodities there. You would be content to live poorly and lowly in this world so that you might have your riches when you come into your mansions of glory.

Seventh, tradesmen who trade for great matters must trust much. They cannot expect to have present pay in great sums. It's true, men who trade for little matters trade by retail. They usually take in their pence and two pence as their commodities go forth. But it's not so with merchants who trade for great things in wholesale. Traders for heaven trust much and, indeed, the grace of faith is the great grace that helps in the trading for heaven; they have a little earnest for the present.

You who are traders and go to the exchange and sell bargains for many thousands, you may not have more than twelve pence or a crown for the present, the first fruits of the Spirit, or a bare promise from Christ. This is that which binds the whole bargain, and they expect to have the full pay hereafter when they come to heaven. It is a happy thing when God gives men and women hearts to be willing to trust God for eternity; and if they have just a little comfort and grace now, they ought to look at that as an earnest penny of all the glory that Jesus Christ has purchased by His blood and that God has promised in His Word. You are not fit to be a tradesman for heaven if you cannot trust, if you cannot be content that great bargains should be bound with a little earnest. But that's the soul that trades in heaven, that can be content to wait for the fulfilling of the promises, and to take what they have from God for the present, though it is but a very little, as an earnest to bind all those glorious things that God has promised in His Word. Here you see a trader for heaven in these seven things. Now put all these things together with what you have heard previously and you may see what it is to have our conversations in heaven.

CHAPTER EIGHT

Seven Evidences of Men's Having Their Conversation in Heaven

There are some evidences of Christians having their conversation in heaven. As we showed you some evidences of an earthly conversation, so likewise of a heavenly conversation, that is, some demonstrations to show plainly that the conversations of Christians are in heaven.

1. It's certainly plain that there are Christians who have their conversations in heaven. First, because there are Christians who can vilify all the things of this earth. Unless they had their conversations higher than the earth they could not so vilify the things of the earth. It's an evidence of the height of heaven that a man is lifted up very high and shall look upon the very globe of the earth as a little thing. So it is an evidence that the hearts of the saints are on high when they can look upon the earth as small. It's true that we who are on the earth look upon the stars as small and the earth as great; but if we were in heaven we would look upon the stars as great and the earth as small as Paul did. He accounted all things as dung

and dross, dog meat, for the excellency of the knowledge of Jesus Christ. Luther accounted the whole Turkish empire as a crumb that the great Master of the family casts to His dog. Here's an argument that the saints have their conversations in heaven, that they can look upon the things of the earth as so low and so little, as indeed they are.

2. A second evidence is that they can be content with so little in this world and can live such comfortable lives in the enjoyment of so little. Perhaps you cannot tell how to have comfortable lives unless you have so much coming in each year, so much provision. But one who is heavenly, a godly man or woman, can tell how to live a joyful and happy life in the lack of the things of this world. Though they have only a little, just bread and water, mean habitations, mean clothes, low esteem in the world, they can still go through the world with a joyful heart, blessing God all their days, doing nothing but admiring, praising, and magnifying God for His rich mercy, and blessing himself in God, accounting his portion to be a good portion and his lot to be fallen into a fair ground.

I truly believe that there are many poor, low people in this world whose houses are filled with more of the blessings of God in one day than many rich, great, noble men have in twenty or forty years. This argues that they have their conversations in heaven, that though they lack comfort in this world, yet they can live comfortable lives. Surely it is something that causes them to rejoice, when they can rejoice in the lack of these outward things, when their joy does not depend on the things of this world. If men who have earthly hearts lose even their outward comforts they cry out, "Oh, we are undone!" And you might see mighty alterations in their very countenances. They have nothing to cheer their hearts when they lose the things of the world; but it is not so with the saints. Whatever crosses they meet with in this world, yet they still rejoice in Christ, blessing God. The course of their lives is nothing but a continual magnifying and praising God for His mercy and goodness to them. Surely they have their conversations in heaven.

Not only can they live joyfully in the lack of many comforts, but they can suffer the loss of all, yea, suffer hard things, suffer afflictions, suffer torments and tortures with joyful hearts. Just read Hebrews 11:13–14 at your leisure: "They confessed that they were strangers and pilgrims on the earth, for they that seek such things declare plainly that they seek a country."

Mark it. They who seek such things declare plainly that they seek a country. Surely there is something else that they seek after when they set so lightly on the things of this world, for the saints are not fools. There is some reason for what they do; surely there is something in it. For they have the same nature as you have; they have need of comfort as well as you and, had they not some other comfort besides outward comforts, they could not live so comfortably in the lack of outward comforts. But they who are content with a little as pilgrims and strangers plainly declare that they seek a country.

3. Another evidence is the suffering of tortures and pains for the sake of Christ. Hebrews 10:32–33: "But call to remembrance the former days in which after ye were illuminated ye endured a great fight of affliction, partly, while ye were made a gazing stock, both by reproaches and afflictions, and partly while ye became companions of them to were so used." And then in verse 34: "And took joyfully the spoiling of your goods." Why? "Knowing in yourselves that ye have in heaven a better and enduring substance." This made them take the spoiling of their goods joyfully.

What? When their goods were spoiled, did they take that joyfully? Were they madmen to rejoice at the plundering of their estates? No, it was not madness; it was because they knew that they had in heaven a better and an enduring substance, and that made them willing to wander about in sheepskins and goatskins, in leather clothes. In the latter end of Hebrews 11, read from these verses to the end. This proves that their conversations were in heaven. If you read the stories of the martyrs, you shall often find that when they came to the stake their thoughts and their hearts were in heaven, and they encouraged one another as to what they should have in heaven, and of the glory that they would have there. Being willing to suffer such things for Christ, and being able to undergo all with so much joy, is an evidence that there have been Christians in the world who have had their conversations in heaven.

4. A fourth evidence of Christians having their conversations in heaven is that their hearts are so filled with heavenly riches. If a man tells me he is a merchant, but not of which country, and I come to his warehouse and see it filled with Spanish or Turkish commodities, I may conclude with certainty that this man is a Spanish or Turkish merchant. He has the commodities of the country continually in his warehouse. So, the saints have much of the riches of heaven in their hearts continually. They have much grace, much holiness, much of the image of God, much spiritual life. You may see in his conversation that he manifests much of the excellency of heaven, for much of the glory of heaven shines in his face. Surely his conversation is in heaven who has so much of the riches of heaven in his heart.

"The heart of the wicked," says the Holy Ghost, "is worth little." Look into the heart of a wicked man or woman. What is there? Your heart should be your storehouse, and what is it filled with? It's filled with dirt, dross, filth, and uncleanness. The hearts of wicked men are stored with those things. But now look into the hearts of the saints. They are filled with

God, with Christ, with the Holy Ghost, with grace. That shows you they have traded much in heaven. In a constant way you shall find their hearts filled with grace, and you shall see them manifesting much grace in their lives. Therefore, surely their conversation is in heaven.

5. A fifth evidence is that they are willing to purchase the privileges of heaven at so dear a rate, namely the ordinances that are part of the privileges of the kingdom of heaven. Now, they are willing to purchase, at a dear rate, the ordinances that are the means whereby men come to enjoy so much of heaven. Oh, however I live, let me live where I may enjoy the ordinances of God, the wells of salvation! My life cannot be comfortable in the enjoyment of all the things in this world if I should be deprived of the breasts of consolation. Surely they who are willing to purchase heavenly commodities at so dear a rate, as the saints will do, declare their conversation to be in heaven.

6. It is evidence when they are so sensible of the stoppages between heaven and their own soul. If there should be a general stoppage of ships that are in France, Turkey, or Spain, your average person would not be aware of it at all. But your merchants, I'll bet, would be aware and, when they come together at the exchange, their talk would be of it. So it is with those who have their conversations in heaven. Here's a great difference between those men and earthly-minded men. Tell those who are earthly of any stoppage in the intercourse between them and heaven and they will not know what you mean; they will think you are a fool or mad. But the saints are sensible of it. Oh, it is a sore and sad evil to them when at any time God hides His face from them, when at any time they go into the presence of God and hear nothing from Him, receive no letters from heaven!

If the mail does not come from such and such a country,

the merchants are troubled by it. So when the saints send up their prayers to heaven by which they trade there, and can hear nothing from God in return, when they cannot feel those influences from heaven let into their souls as heretofore they have sometimes done, oh, they bewail this as a great evil that is upon them! It is a greater evil than any evil in the world that the influences of heaven are stopped, and that God seems to be a stranger unto them. These things they complain of to one another, and they moan when they feel the stoppages of heaven. This plainly declares that they are traders for heaven, and that their conversations are there.

7. The last evidence of a saint's having his conversation in heaven is his willingness to die, to depart this world, going out of this world with so much comfort, joy, peace, and triumph, as many of the saints have done. We might give you the expressions of many of the saints when they were ready to die, rejoicing at the hope of eternal life at their going out of the world. Surely had they not conversed in heaven while they lived here, their souls would not have been so willing to have departed out of their bodies.

A man who has nothing to do in another country is like a dead man there; he goes there with little joy. But a man who has been trading in another country and has great riches and has thrived there, whatever he seems to be here, he is a great man there! Oh, how comfortably that man goes to that country!

How glad he is when he takes ship and sees a fair gale and prosperous winds to carry him to that country! And so it is with the saints who have their conversation in heaven, because they have so many riches there that when they come to die they die with joy, and bless God for that day as the most blessed day they have seen; for now they are going to the country they have been trading in all their days and where their riches lie. These are the evidences and demonstrations that the saints have their conversations in heaven.

CHAPTER NINE

Four Reasons Why the Saints Have Their Conversation in Heaven

If you demand the reason why it is that the saints have their conversation in heaven, I will answer briefly this way:

REASON 1. Because their souls, their better part, are from heaven. You know that when God made man He breathed into his nostrils the breath of life. The soul of man is, as it were, the breath of God. God did not say of man's soul, as He did of other creatures, "Let it be made; let there be a soul in man's body." No, rather, when He had formed the body He breathed His soul into him. That was to note that the soul of man had a more heavenly and divine origin than any of the other creatures in this world. Because the origin is so divine and heavenly, therefore, when the soul is set at liberty it will be as its origins. Indeed, though man's soul is of a divine and heavenly nature, through the fall of man the soul of man is almost turned to flesh, and it is so mingled with unclean drossy things as if it had no such origins.

Therefore, a natural man is called flesh. "That which is born of the flesh is flesh," as if it had no soul at all. The nature of the soul of man, through the fall, has changed so, and is depressed down to such vile things, it is as if it never had such a divine and heavenly origin. But now, when God works grace in the soul, the soul of man begins to return to itself and know itself. It begins to return to its own nature, the one it had in its first creation. As soon as the soul begins to know itself it looks at all these things that are here below as vile things in comparison, as contemptible; for all these things in this world are infinitely beneath the soul of man by comparison. We may even call it an infinite distance between man's soul and all these things that are here below in the world. The soul of man is near unto God Himself; and therefore when the soul returns to itself, it would be somewhere other than where it is, and would converse with those things that are suitable to its origins.

It would be the same with a man of noble birth. Suppose a prince was taken to another country and there, being a child, is used like a slave, set to dig ditches and such low employment. All the while he is there, not knowing his origins, he minds nothing but to get his food and do his work. But once he comes to know where he came from, namely born the heir to a great prince or emperor who lives in so much glory, then he who lived like a slave has his thoughts and mind and longings to be in the country where his was a high birth. Oh, that he might be there! He would be happy then, and it does him good to hear any man speak of that country!

Truly, so it is with the souls of men. They are the birth of the high God, of the great King of heaven and earth, who has breathed into the nostrils of man. Now, through man's fall, the soul comes to be a slave to the devil and is set about drudgery to provide for the flesh. But when God is pleased to convert the soul, the Lord comes to declare to a man or woman, "O man, woman! You are born from on high! Your soul is, as it were, a sparkle of the divinity of your Father by creation," not only by creation, as God is the Creator of all creatures, but by a more special work of His, by a more special work than in the first creation of other things.

Your soul is from God, of a divine nature, and is, therefore, capable of communion with Father, Son, and Holy Ghost. Certainly you never had such a divine and excellent being given to you merely that you should delight in the flesh and be subject to your body in eating and drinking here for a while. Oh, think of that country from whence you came at first. Here's one work of grace, to know the excellency of our souls and from whence they came. Surely, if grace does this, it must warm the heart of one that is converted to God, to have his conversation be in heaven. That's the first reason.

REASON 2. Because the soul had a heavenly origin, it will not be content with a portion in this world; but, second, when grace comes there, the soul has a divine nature put into it that goes beyond the excellency of its first creation. There is a divine nature higher than mere natural excellency. 2 Peter 1:3–4: "According as His divine power hath given unto us all things that pertain to life and godliness, and whereby are given unto us exceeding great and precious promises, that by these you might be partakers of the divine nature." Certainly the apostle did not mean here merely what Adam had in innocence. I've never heard that called "the divine nature," though it's true there is a renewing of the image of God in man when he is converted. But there is something more in the soul of man than this. The Holy Ghost comes and dwells in the soul in a higher way than it dwelled in the soul of Adam.

Before man was a creature, but such a creature who could only relate to God in the sense that God was the Creator and man was the creature. But now man can relate to God as being made one with the second Person in the Trinity, and so one with the Father, and therefore of a higher nature than man was in the state of innocence. You know what was said of Adam in paradise, that he was of the earth, earthly. He was of the earth in comparison to the second Adam, and even if Adam had stood firm his posterity would have been earthly. We never read in Scripture that Adam would have been in a heavenly condition had he stood firm; but the second Adam was from heaven, heavenly. And the posterity of the second Adam, those who are made the children of the everlasting Father by regeneration, those who are made the posterity of Jesus Christ by faith, are from heaven, heavenly. Therefore, their souls are endued with a divine nature, with such high principles of grace that it carries their souls up to heaven.

If a lump of earth should be so changed as to have a spirit and life put into it, and made of such an aerial nature as the birds are, this lump of earth would fly in the air. It is so in the work of conversion. All men and women are earthly, and therefore they sink down to the earth. The earth is their proper center; but when they come to be converted there is a spirit put into them whereby they come to mount up aloft. It is no more natural for the earth to fall down low than it is for the fire and air to ascend high, because every creature moves toward its center. Heavy things fall down because below is the proper place for them; light things rise up because their proper place is above. And so the conversation of the saints must be in heaven because that's their center; that which is suitable to the divine nature is put into them.

REASON 3. Their conversations must be in heaven because those things that are the most choice things to them are in heaven. I should have named a great many particulars here to show what are the choice things that concern the saints, and how they are all in heaven. Their Father, God, is in heaven. "Our Father, which art in heaven." Jesus Christ is in heaven. "Seek the things above where Jesus Christ is sitting at the right hand of the Father." Jesus Christ, who is their Head, is in heaven. Their Husband is in heaven, their Elder Brother is in heaven, their King is in heaven, their treasure is in heaven, their inheritance is in heaven, their hope is in heaven, their mansion is in heaven, their chief friends are in heaven, their substance is in heaven, their reward is in heaven, and their wages are in heaven. All these things being in heaven; it is no wonder that their conversations are in heaven.

And they are going to heaven. Now since they are going that way, traveling to heaven, they must be there in their hearts. Heaven is the place they shall come to before long. They shall be there, and they know that they will only be here in this world a little while, but there they will be forever, "We shall be caught up into the clouds and be forever with Him."

Their conversations must be in heaven for they have much of heaven already. There's much of heaven in the saints. The kingdom of heaven is within them, says the Scriptures. They, having so much of heaven, must have their conversations there, for so says the Scripture in Hebrews 10:34: "Knowing in yourselves that ye have in heaven a better and enduring substance." You may read it this way, "knowing you have heaven, a better and enduring substance in yourselves." So that the words, "knowing in yourselves," have reference not only to what they know by hearsay, but what they know in themselves. (It is true, though, that they may know heaven by hearsay, for they hear ministers speak of heaven, and they read it in the Word of God.) They know it by what God has revealed in their own hearts, though they are not book-learned, and though they cannot read a letter in the book, though they hear no more sermons. By what is revealed in themselves, they know in themselves that they have a better and more enduring substance. That's true, but the words may be more proper in the original read thusly: "Knowing that you have heaven in yourselves, a better and enduring substance." Eternal life has already begun in the hearts of the saints. There is heaven already in the saints; and therefore it is no wonder that their conversations are in heaven.

REASON 4. God has so ordered things in this world, on purpose, that He might wean the hearts of the saints from this world. The Lord loves to have the hearts of His saints to be in heaven where He has treasured up such glorious things for them. And because of that, the saints, while they are here in the world and have so much of the world in them, are reluctantly living in this world. Therefore, God so orders things that they will meet with little to content them in this world, so they will be weary of it and wearied by it. Indeed, here's the reason why God's people have met with such crosses in the world, why the Lord has kept His saints so low and mean in the world.

It may be that you are ready to draw bad conclusions from this, and to think, "I am afraid God does not love me, because He keeps me so low and mean. I meet with such crosses and others do not." Oh, do not gather such bad conclusions as these! It is because He would gather your hearts to heaven and wean you from the world, so that you might long to be with Him in heaven. For you are absent from Him here in this world, and the Lord would have the full stream of your affections to run after those things that you shall have with Him in heaven.

This is the use you are to make of those afflictions you meet with, and those crosses that befall you in this world. And thus we have gone through the doctrinal point of the saints having their conversations in heaven.

CHAPTER TEN

The First Use

W e have long treated that point of a heavenly conversation, and have opened to you what that heavenly conversation is, and wherein it consists, in many particulars. Now we shall proceed to the application of all of this. As I have gone along I have endeavored not only to speak to your heads, but your hearts, and to quicken what I have said so that it might quicken your hearts. Still, from the consideration of all, there are divers uses that may be profitable to you.

USE 1. If the saints live such a heavenly conversation as has been opened to you, oh, how far are they from being saints, from being godly, who are so far from having their conversations in heaven as they have their conversations in hell! There is a generation of men who profess themselves to be Christians and say they hope to go to heaven. Yet, if you behold their conversation, it is none other than the conversation of hell. Certainly it is not what men say, but how they live that will cause them to fall another day. He who is of heaven, or for heaven, has his conversation in heaven. He who is for hell has a hellish conversation. Now that is a hellish conversation that is like that which is done in hell. What is there in hell but blaspheming and cursing? What is there in hell but hatred and malice? What is there in hell but raging and filthiness? These things are the conversations of many men who are even devils incarnate!

In many families the name of God is blasphemed. There's cursing and railing, malice, wrath, and pride, so that though they are here in this world, they manifest to which place they belong. The saints have their conversations in heaven, and when they die they go to their own place, that is, to heaven where their conversations were. On the contrary, when the wicked die, having their conversations in hell, they go to their own place. It was said of Judas, "He went to his own place." When a wicked man dies who had his conversation in hell while he lived, he goes to his own place; that's his own proper place. He found his delight and contentment in those things that were done there; so when he dies, it is there he shall go. "As the tree falls, so it lies." Since your conversation is there, and the bent of your heart is there, so it must lie there to all eternity.

Chapter Eleven

The Second Use

USE 2. This point, likewise, rebukes hypocrites as wicked, profane ones who have their conversations in hell. There's another kind of men that are unsound professors, hypocrites who have their conversations between heaven and earth. It's not in heaven, nor is it in hell, nor altogether on the earth, but between earth, heaven, and hell. Sometimes they seem to be aloft, above. Sometimes they are very forward and zealous in the profession of religion, sometimes much enlarged in duties. At other times they are as base, earthly spirits as any. Yea, sometimes, there's much of hell in their hearts and in their ways. They profess themselves to be the seed of Abraham, but they are not as the stars of heaven, but as the meteors that are between heaven and earth. We call them blazing stars. They are not as bright as the stars, nor are they of such a heavy nature as the stars. They are made of a few unclean vapors that come out of the earth which, having gotten up near the heavens, make a show as if they were some star from heaven. But you will find a great deal of difference between the stars and them in this, for within a little while they fall, vanish, and come to nothing.

So it is with many hypocrites: by the Word they are raised up a little for the present and seem to be above the stars. They have a glittering show as if they had something heavenly in them, even like the stars of heaven. They seem to have gotten higher than others. A child would think a blazing star to be a great deal bigger than one of the stars that is a hundred times bigger. So it is with hypocrites: they have a greater show of religion than many who have the truth of God and who are truly gracious. They wonder at the excellent parts that they have, excellent abilities it may be. They will discourse sometimes in an excellent manner about heavenly things. You shall find some who have no soundness at all, yet will have very excellent discourse. They speak the very language of Canaan, but it is in such company where they may gain respect by it.

Still, they are just meteors that hang between heaven and earth, whereas the truth is, while they seem to be so high above others and so heavenly, their hearts are still groveling upon the earth.

They have, many times, the most excellent expressions in prayer; yet God sees their hearts basely cleaving to some earthly things. There is some base, earthly contentment their hearts are upon while they seem to be so heavenly. It is much like the hawk that flies on high as if it were an eagle, but while it flies its eye is fixed upon some prey that it has on the earth. As soon as it sees a fit opportunity to seize its prey it comes down to seize it. That's where the hawk would be; that's the place he most delights in, to be upon his prey. And so a hypocrite, though he rises high in some actions, the truth is, his eye is upon some earthly prey; and when he sees his opportunity, there he goes and sinks down to those things. That's his proper place; there he takes most delight and content in his conversation, though his actions may seem so heavenly. Therefore, he will fall down and never attain to the highest heavens to which the saints shall go, but to hell at last.

CHAPTER TWELVE

The Third Use

USE 3. Is the saint's conversation in heaven? Then for shame; let us not find fault with strictness in the ways of God. Let not man speak against the ways of God as being too strict. What need do we have to be so circumspect, so precise, and so pure? What need do we have to labor so much? What! Can you attain to a more strict and holy conversation than a heavenly conversation? It is a very carnal expression that some have, "Why, we cannot be saints? We are not saints." Yes, the Holy Ghost calls all believers who have the very least degree of true grace saints. When we come to heaven, then we shall live better; but while we are in this world we cannot. Yes, while you are in this world your conversation is to be in heaven. Either men are not acquainted with the Word, or they shut their eyes and will not see and consider what the Word says about a strict conversation.

Sometimes you find in Scripture that we are commanded to be perfect as our heavenly Father is perfect. It's a strange speech, but it is the speech of Christ Himself; and we must walk as Christ walked. He who has this hope purifies himself as He is pure. Then our conversation is in heaven. Put these together: perfect as our Heavenly Father is perfect and walk as Christ walked, purge ourselves as He is pure. Our conversation is in heaven. What do all these things lead to? Surely they lead to a great deal of strictness and holiness of life. And these things show that the work of a Christian here in this world is a busy work, that a Christian life is not an idle, dull, heavy, or sluggish life.

You who are Christians need to quicken yourselves. You need to awaken those drowsy spirits of yours. If it is required of you that you be perfect as your Heavenly Father is perfect, walk as Christ walked, purify yourselves as He is pure, be holy as He is holy, and to have your conversations in heaven, surely there must be a great deal of quickness and life in the hearts of Christians. You are not to content yourselves in a mere profession, doing some little matter in the way of religion, or being somewhat better than others; you are to aim at heaven. Look up there and make that to be your pattern.

CHAPTER THIRTEEN

The Fourth Use

USE 4. This rebukes even such as are truly godly, yet who fail much in this. Oh, their conversations are too low, too earthly! If they would examine their hearts strictly, they could not say that their conversations are in heaven. "I am a stranger on earth," said David. But many may say that they are strangers in heaven, whereas earth should be the place of our pilgrimage and heaven our home. But it's quite otherwise; heaven is rather the place where most professors are strange and earth is the place of their habitation. They cast up a thought now and then to heaven, as now and then men will cast up their eyes and look upon heaven, but where's your heart? Where are the great workings of your spirits? It's a speech of our Lord, "Heaven is My throne, and earth is My footstool." Spiritual things are to be looked upon as the good things, as the throne of God, and those earthly things only as the things of God's footstool. But now, how many are there who have earth as their throne and heaven their footstool? That is, heavenly things are made subordinate to earthly things.

This should not be in any of those who profess themselves to be Christians. None of the saints should satisfy themselves in any life but this: to be able to say, "I bless God that my conversation is in heaven. Though God lets me live on the earth, my conversation is in heaven." What an unworthy thing it is for one who professes to have his portion and inheritance in heaven to have his heart so mingled here with the earth. In Genesis 45:20, Joseph said in sending for his father, "Regard not your stuff, for the good of all the land of Egypt is yours."

"Regard not your stuff." Do not let it grieve you to forsake your stuff. Leave all your lumber behind you, for all the good things of Egypt are yours. Oh, what a shameful thing it is that Christians should regard their stuff as much as they do, who hope to have the good things, not of Egypt, but of heaven itself to be theirs! Surely, if we had seen the things of heaven, one would think that all the things of the earth would be darkened in our eyes. We would see "that which was glorious had no glory in comparison of the greater glory" (2 Corinthians 3:10). That Scripture, I confess, is spoken comparing the law and the gospel. There was a glory in the delivering of the law, but not in comparison to the greater glory, not in comparison to the gospel. For in the gospel "we behold as in a glass with open face, the glory of God, and are changed into the same image as from glory to glory."

But we may apply it thus. Things of the earth that were glorious in your eyes before should not at all be glorious in comparison to the greater glory. Though before conversion these things were glorious (and I grant that there is some kind of glory upon the things of this world, that they are gilded and varnished over), yet in comparison to the greater glory, they are not glorious at all. You who have seen the greater glory should not account earthly things glorious. Oh, therefore, Christians, lift up your hearts to heaven and let your conversation be in heaven, even though God has so ordered that you must live here awhile, and must be content!

To some Christians who have their conversations in heaven, it's a great part of their self-denial, and of their subjection to God, to be willing to live upon the earth, and to stay away from heaven until God's time comes. This is a riddle and a mystery to many, that obedience and self-denial should be a part of our salvation. Though they had crowns of glory, though they were kings and princes in this world, they should be willing to stay here. We might come to attain this if our conversations were in heaven, and our hearts there.

We read of Daniel that though God ordered that he could not live at Jerusalem where the temple was, yet he would open his window towards Jerusalem; he would always be looking that way. And so, though God has so ordered that we cannot yet come to live in that heavenly Jerusalem bodily, and in that full way as we expect to do hereafter, yet we should open our windows; our eyes, and the doors of our hearts should be opened towards heaven. I can remember reading of Edward the First, King of England, who had a mind to go to Jerusalem; but because he could not go, death preventing him, he gave charge to his son to carry his heart there. And so it should be with us: we should endeavor to have our hearts there, and to have as much of heaven as we can, though we cannot be there ourselves bodily. God has placed within every creature an instinct to move to its proper place. Because the proper place of fire is above, the instinct of nature in fire is to ascend to its proper place. And the proper place of earth is below and, therefore, it will fall down to the center.

A heavy thing that has much earth in it, though it breaks itself to pieces, still will fall down towards its center. And so it will be with a Christian: though he breaks himself into pieces, whatever he suffers he has an instinct to carry him to his proper place. Because the proper place of fire is above, even if it is kept down by violence, what a mighty power there is in fire that makes a way for it to get up. That's the very reason for the mighty force there is in guns, because there is fire in the powder that is kept in. Once the powder is fired (because the fire would get up above) it breaks out with violence; and if it cannot get out it breaks anything in the world, for it must get out to get to its own place. And so it should be with a Christian. There should be a strong impetuousness to get to his own place; that would be an evidence that heaven is your proper place. O Christians, lift up your hearts and let your conversations be in heaven!

CHAPTER FOURTEEN

A Heavenly Conversation Is a Convincing Conversation

I shall not need to tell you again what heavenly conversation is; it has been opened at large to you. But to set an edge on this exhortation know that a heavenly conversation will be a very convincing conversation. You will convince men that you have something more than they have when they see you live heavenly lives. The men of the world know that the things of the world are the things their hearts are set upon, those that they mind. When they see those who profess religion mingling themselves with the earth as they do, then they will think that they act on the same principles. But heavenly conversations will convince them when they behold men walking above in the whole course of their lives, when they see an evenness and proportion in their course. If you were to see them at any time in their businesses, they carry themselves as men of another world. A man who is a stranger to a place may act like a native, but one who was born in that place will find him out in something. So, it is very hard for men to carry themselves so if they do not have true grace, though they appear sometimes to be very heavenly. One who is a true citizen of heaven will discern whether they have grace or not at one time or another.

The truth is, a carnal man will reveal himself to be born of the earth. His speech betrays him to be a Giliadite. But when Christians shall constantly have their conversations in heaven, then their conversations are very convincing. There are the rays of heaven about them; they have the luster of heaven shining wherever they go, and in all company. Surely such a man seems to be in heaven continually. It will force the very consciences of men to say, "Certainly these are the citizens of heaven. If there are any denizens of the New Jerusalem while they live upon the earth, these are they."

I remember that it is said of that martyr, Dr. Taylor, that he rejoiced that he ever came into the prison to be in the company of that angel of God, Mr. Bradford. Mr. Bradford's conversations were angelic, like an angel of heaven, and convinced almost everyone wherever he went. Oh, 'tis of great use that Christians should live convincing conversations. You know what Dives said to Abraham, that he desired to have one sent to warn his brethren that they might not come to that place. Abraham said, "They have Moses and the prophets." But Dives said, "If one rises from the dead, they would hear him." I may say this, if God should send one from heaven to live among men and to preach to them, surely they would regard him. Would it not be a great benefit to the world if God should send a saint from heaven, or an angel, to converse in a bodily way among us? Truly, Christians should live as if they came from heaven every day, as if they had been in heaven conversing with God. When they go to perform their duties in the morning and get alone with God and their souls, they should never stop striving until they get their hearts in heaven and themselves upon the mount, so that when they come down to their families, their very faces should shine, so that you might see by their conversations that they certainly have been with God upon the mount this day.

Now I appeal to you in this, do you live so that your family and neighbors can see that you have been in heaven this morning? Every morning we should have a talk with heaven; and, if we did, our conversations would be convincing all the day long, and it would be very profitable to the world. Christians who live heavenly conversations are of great use in the places where they live. It's said of Christ that when He ascended up to heaven He gave gifts to men. If we would ascend more often to heaven, we would be more beneficial to the world.

CHAPTER FIFTEEN

A Heavenly Conversation Is Growing

A heavenly conversation is a growing conversation. Oh, they grow mightily! They thrive in grace a great deal in a very short time; they grow to attain to a very great measure of communion with God the Father and with Jesus Christ. And every day they grow more and more spiritual, having so much of heaven within them. It's true, when they come to heaven they shall be perfect, but now the fetching from heaven is that which makes them grow. It is the influence of heaven that causes the growth of the saints. Suppose that the ground upon which flowers and herbs grow is not fertile in itself, and the herbs or plants are not rooted well in the earth. If there is not an influence of heaven upon them they will not grow much, no, not at all, but rather will quickly wither.

So it is with Christians. Let them have the means of growth and many ordinances, yet if they do not have rich dews from above they will not grow. Or if there is any growth, either they will bear no fruit or else it will be very shriveled and sour fruit. The fruit that has the most of the sun grows riper and sweeter than other fruits. Fruit that grows in the shade, that has the influence of heaven kept from it, is sour fruit. The reason that the saints have so little fruit, and that it is so sour, is because they do not have more influences from heaven. They do not stand in the open sun, their souls are not presented daily before God. They do not have the warm beams of the sun of righteousness shining from heaven upon them. But there is something between heaven and their souls.

A conversation in heaven, as it would be a convincing conversation, must be a growing conversation.

CHAPTER SIXTEEN

A Heavenly Conversation Brings Much Glory to God

A heavenly conversation would be a conversation glorifying God a great deal. Oh, the glory that God would have from a conversation in heaven! Let your light so shine before men that others, beholding your good works, may glorify your Father who is in heaven. Then, indeed, the image of the God of heaven is held forth when men's conversations are heavenly. The Lord takes much delight in having His glory dispensed abroad by the saints, to have some reflection on the world. It is as with a glass. Though beams of the sun do not shine upon a wall, yet by a glass you may take the beams of the sun and cast a reflection of them upon a wall. So those beams of the glory of God that shine in heaven are. The saints by their heavenly conversation may, as it were, take them and reflect them upon the world and the faces of men. The hearts of the saints should be as a glass, taking the beams of the glory of God and casting them up and down where they are; and so your heavenly Father should come to be glorified by you.

Let every Christian think thus: "My conversation is thus and thus. But what glory do I bring to God by my conversation?

Do others glorify God by beholding the luster of the holiness of God in me? Do they see any cause to bless God that they see so much of the glory of God in me?" Certainly, there is more of the glory of God shining in the gracious, holy, spiritual conversation of a Christian than shines in the sun, moon, and stars, than in heaven and earth. I mean the works of creation and providence that are in heaven and earth, the creatures that God has made, like the sun, moon, and stars, and here in this world, the seas, the earth, the plants, and the like, though they have much of the glory of God, yet a heavenly conversation declares more of the glory of God than all these.

You know what the Psalmist said, "The heavens declare the glory of God, and the firmament shows His handiwork." It may be spoken more fully of heavenly conversations. The heavenly conversations of the saints declare the glory of God; and those who shine in the firmament of the church are stars, and they declare the handiwork of God. The church is the firmament and the saints are there as stars. Now though this is true, in heaven one star differs from another in glory, and in Christianity, every one cannot attain to as much glory as another. But every one is a star; the lowest Christian who lives, the weakest believer there is, is still as a star in the firmament, though he cannot shine as gloriously as the sun or as other stars. There should never be a believer, never a godly man or woman in the church, who does not shine as a star in the firmament, who should not be as the gospel is, a mirror wherein we may behold the glory of God, in whom we may behold the glory of God even, as it were, with open face. A heavenly conversation is a conversation glorifying to God.

Chapter Seventeen

A Heavenly Conversation Brings Much Glory to the Saints

heavenly conversation is one that will bring much glory to yourselves. Though it's true that the saints should aim at the glory of God most, there will come glory upon themselves whether they wish it or not if their conversations are in heaven. It's impossible for the consciences of men not to be honored if they are walking in a heavenly conversation. There's an excellent Scripture that shows that in glorifying God we glorify ourselves. In 2 Thessalonians 1:11–12, the apostle prays for them: "Wherefore also we pray always for you, that our God would count you worthy of this calling, and fulfill all the good pleasure of His goodness, and the work of faith with power." To what end? "That the name of our Lord Jesus Christ may be glorified in you, and you in Him, according to the grace of our God, and the Lord Jesus Christ."

He prays for the Thessalonians that they might walk so that they might have so much of the grace of God in them, that the name of our Lord Jesus Christ might be glorified in them. Oh, this is that which all the saints should desire and endeavor after, that the name of our Lord Jesus Christ should be glorified in them, and you in Him, he says. Labor that Christ may have glory in our glory, and then we shall have glory in Christ's glory. This is a sweet and blessed life when the saints have such hearts that they can say, "Lord, let me have no glory, but that you may have glory in." Then God says, "Is it so? Do you desire no further glory in this world but that I may have glory in? Then I will have no glory in this world but what you shall have glory in!" Christ will make us partakers of His glory as well as we shall make Him partaker of our glory. Oh, heavenly conversation that glorifies God will glorify the saints, too!

CHAPTER EIGHTEEN

ℐ Heavenly Conversation Will Make Suffering Easy

heavenly conversation will make all sufferings very easy. It will be nothing to suffer anything you meet with in this world if your conversations are in heaven. All revilings, reproaches, and wrongs will be nothing if you just get a heavenly conversation. You will condemn all these things that the men of the world think to be such great matters. Men who have conversed in heaven will never be very offended for any sufferings. 2 Corinthians 4:17: "For our light afflictions, which are but for a moment, worketh for us a far more exceeding and eternal weight of glory; while we look not at the things which are seen, but at things which are not seen; for the things which are seen are temporal, but the things which are seen are eternal."

All are but light afflictions. Why? For our eye is above all these things. And it's a notable passage in the gospels, if you examine the place of Christ's transfiguration upon the mount where Christ showed His glory unto some disciples He took with Him. Observe in the story who the disciples were who Christ took with Him to see His glory: they were Peter, James, and John. Compare that story with the story of Christ in His agony. His soul was heavy unto death. He was to be betrayed and crucified the next day. He fell groveling upon the earth and, sweating great drops of blood through the anguish that was upon His spirit, cried out, "O Lord! If it be possible, let this cup pass from Me." There's a great difference between Christ in His agony and Christ upon the Mount of Transfiguration. And observe that Christ would have none of His disciples see Him in His agony but Peter, James, and John, only those three who saw Him in His transfiguration upon the mount in His glory.

The note from this is that those who can converse much with Christ in glory can converse with Christ in heaven, can see heaven, may be permitted to see Christ in His agony, and it will do them no harm. The other disciples who did not see Christ in His glory, had they seen Christ in His agony might have been offended. "Is this our Lord and Master that is in such a fearful agony at this time?" Oh, it would have offended them! But those who saw Him glorified were not offended. "Though He is in agony now, still we know Him to be a glorious Savior, and we will believe and trust in Him still."

So, if we can converse with God in glory upon the mount, whatever agony we see Christ in afterwards we shall be able to bear it. Stephen saw the stones go flying by his ears but, when he saw the heavens opened, it was nothing to him. He fell asleep; he rejoiced in the expectation of heaven. If you read the *Book of Martyrs*, whenever they came to suffer you see how they rejoiced when they thought of heaven and remembered eternal life. A child was about to be burned, and the people expected the mother to wring her hands and make great lamentations to see her child stepping into the flames; but she said nothing but this, "Remember eternal life, my son." Oh, conversing with heaven makes all sufferings in the world to be nothing!

$\mathcal{A}$ Heavenly Conversation Brings Much Joy

$\mathcal{O}$h, the sweetness and comfort there will be while the soul is conversing in heaven! Oh, the joy and peace that will come to the soul in the certain evidence that it is a partaker in the death, resurrection, and intercession of Jesus Christ! Those whose conversations are in heaven come to have certain evidence to their souls because they have their portion in the death, resurrection, ascension, and intercession of Jesus Christ, and this will afford comfort enough. Colossians 3:1: "If ye be risen with Christ, seek those things that are above where Christ sitteth on the right hand of God; set your affections on things above, not on things on the earth, for ye are dead and your life is hid with Christ in God. When Christ, who is our life, shall appear, then shall ye also appear with Him in glory."

This is an evidence that you are risen with Christ: when you are dead to the world, and have an interest in His ascension, and are partakers of His resurrection, and have part in His intercession. Those who have their conversations in heaven now may know certainly that they are risen from death to life, that when Christ ascended He went to heaven to take possession for them, yea, that they are in heaven where Christ is. "He hath set us in heavenly places together with Christ Jesus." There is the common head, that they are ascended with Christ already, and that Christ is there as an Advocate, making intercession for them to the Father. These will be the consolations of those who have their conversations in heaven.

CHAPTER TWENTY

A Heavenly Conversation Is Very Safe

A conversation in heaven is a very safe conversation. You will be free from snares and temptations. As an earthly conversation subjects us to temptations, so a heavenly conversation will free us from temptations. When is the bird in danger of the snare or the net except when she comes to pick below upon the ground? But if she could just keep herself above always, she would be safe from the snare and the net. It's Chrysostom's saying, "Keep above, and then ye be free from the snare of the fowler." It's a safe conversation.

CHAPTER TWENTY-ONE

A Heavenly Conversation Gives Abundant Entrance into Glory

t will cause an abundant entrance into the kingdom of heaven. When the saints come to die, oh, how joyfully will they die! What abundant entrance will be made into the everlasting kingdom of our Lord and Savior, Jesus Christ? For when they die, they shall just change their place; they shall not change their company. They shall only go to their Father's house to be partakers of those mansions that Christ has prepared.

O my brethren! Labor to have your conversations in heaven, and know that this is not a matter that only concerns eminent Christians, but all Christians. See how the apostle charges this upon the Thessalonians, in his first epistle, chapter 2:11: "As you know how we exhorted and comforted, and charged every one of you, as a father doth his children, that you would walk worthy of God who hath called you into His kingdom and glory," that is, that you would walk in a conversation suitable to the glorious kingdom of God to which you are called. According to our high calling, we should walk worthy of it. We are charged to do so. It's said of Christ in the Gospel of John that He spoke of Himself as "the Son of Man which is in heaven." So it should be said of every child of God, "such a one who is in heaven," not only such a one who shall go to heaven, but that is in heaven right now.

CHAPTER TWENTY-TWO

Seven Rules or Directions How to Get a Heavenly Conversation

You might say, "What should we do to get our conversation to be in heaven? It's an excellent conversation, indeed, oh, that we might attain unto it!"

RULE 1. Be persuaded that it is attainable. Let Christians thus conclude with themselves: "It is possible for me to live a life of heaven while I am upon the earth." There is a heaven to be had. It will mightily stir up the spirit of a Christian if he will believe this. You may live here with God, Christ, His angels, and His saints. There are some who have attained to this, and how have they done so? Not by their own strength, they were men subject to the same infirmities as you. Even Paul himself, who had his conversation in heaven, was subject to many infirmities. But through the strength of Christ he could do all things. He was nothing in himself, though.

Just read Romans 7. Paul said of himself that he was even sold under sin. When he wanted to do good, evil was present with him. He was led captive, and found a law in his members rebelling against the law of his mind. He had many corruptions and was given a prick in the flesh, a messenger of Satan, to humble him. He spoke of this heavenly conversation, not only that he had it, but wrote to the Philippians that they had attained unto it. They were a very spiritual church, but were poor and lowly in respect to others. They did not have the eminent gifts of the Corinthians, and yet the Philippians had their conversations in heaven. Therefore, it is a thing that is attainable.

RULE 2. If you would get your conversation in heaven, labor to keep a clear conscience; keep a heaven in your conscience. Those men who fully defile their consciences lose their intercourse with heaven; and, indeed, the presence of God is tedious to them. They loathe to go into His presence once they have defiled their consciences. If there is a hell in a man's conscience, there will not be a heaven in his conversation. Let men and women labor to keep conscience clean, and a heaven there, and then there will be a heaven in their conversations.

RULE 3. Watch opportunities for heavenly exercises. Though you have much business in the world, watch your time. You who are servants should not neglect your master's business, for you serve God in the work of your master—but you still must watch your opportunities. Get alone, and if your time cannot be long, then let it be frequent. Watch all opportunities for heavenly exercises, for meditation, for prayer, for reading, for conversing with God. Oh, we might get many opportunities to get our souls in heaven if we would just watch! Those who are diligent to watch opportunities for heavenly exercises, and prize opportunities for them, are the men and women who will attain to a heavenly conversation, who do not make it a light matter whether or not they converse with God in holy duties. Christians who would have their conversations in heaven must look for opportunities for heavenly exercises. They eye them as being where much of the joy and comfort of their lives consists.

RULE 4. In the next place, do not forget this. Take heed, and be careful, that you do not rest in formality. Watch to get opportunities, but do not be formal in duties in them. Oh, this will mightily darken your conversations; it will make them very earthly. There will be no beauty in them if you rest in formality in holy performances. There are many Christians who, we hope, have some good underneath yet, growing into a form of religion, never honor their profession. They have little comfort to their own souls; they go on in a dead-hearted condition. They do not know what it is to have communion with God. Oh, beware of that! We are all subject to it by nature, too.

Those who have enlightened consciences dare not but take opportunities for heavenly duties. But then come the temptations of the devil and the corruption of our own hearts. When you have done your task, it's over. You have prayed, yes, but have you been in heaven during that time? What converse did you have with God? Take heed of formality! It will greatly hinder your conversation. A Christian, though weak, can only chatter to God and speak a few broken words and half sentences. Yet, if he does not rest in formality, he may have much converse with God. Others who have excellent parts, but rest in their work, never know what it means to have a conversation in heaven.

RULE 5. Labor to beat down your bodies, that is, take heed of making provision for the flesh; beware of sensual lusts. How did Paul come to have his conversation in heaven? He said, "I beat down my body." The words literally mean "black and blue." He clubbed it down, as if he should say, "This body of mine would draw my heart from spiritual things and make me earthly and sensual. I will keep my body down. I will not give that satisfaction to the flesh and body so as to strengthen any temptation that might draw my heart from spiritual and heavenly things. No, instead I beat down my body." There is no Christian who is heavenly but he must be very careful and watchful over his senses while he lives here, to beat down his body, and so come to have his conversation in heaven.

RULE 6. Labor to be skillful in the mystery of godliness, to draw strength from Jesus Christ in everything you do. My brethren, Christ is Jacob's ladder. When Jacob lay asleep, he saw a ladder on which the angels descended and ascended up to heaven. This ladder of Jacob's is none other than Jesus Christ to Christians, and that ladder must be set up to heaven. If you would go to heaven and converse with heaven, it must be by Jesus Christ. You must be instructed in the mystery of the gospel, in conversing with God through a Mediator. There is such an infinite distance between God and us that, unless we have Christ the Mediator, we can never come to God, nor can God come to us. It is only Christ the Mediator who is the ladder. We have no need to ask, "Who shall go up to heaven to fetch Christ down?" No, we may have Christ in our hearts and set Him up; so we may go up to heaven by His mediation.

When a Christian comes to live in this manner, and is able to say, "What I expect from God, I expect to draw through a Mediator; and all the services I offer to God, I offer them through the hand and heart of Christ," he has much converse with heaven. By Jesus Christ the Mediator I may come up there and present myself, even though no unclean thing may come there. God looks upon the saints, through Christ, as righteous, being clothed with His righteousness. They may come to their Father with boldness, having their Elder Brother's garments upon them. They may come and kneel before the throne of grace every morning for their Father's blessing. It is by Him that we have access unto the Father. Oh, acquaint yourself with the mystery of godliness in drawing all from Christ and offering all to God through Christ. By this, heaven comes down to you; and by this you climb up to heaven. This is Jacob's ladder.

But those men who only look on God in a natural way reason thusly: "All good things come from God," and so they go to prayer: "Lord, we beseech Thee, bless us this day, for all good things come from Thee." They serve God; their consciences tell them they must worship and serve God while they live here. But it is in a dull, natural way. Let me leave this with your hearts: all good comes from God through a Mediator, through Jesus Christ, the second Person of the Trinity, the God-Man. All my services are offered up to God through Him. There is this Mediator, this God-Man, who unites God and me together. By Him, I have acceptance for both my person and my actions. By Him, I have other kinds of blessings than come from God merely as Creator. God, in bounty, bestows upon the creature many good things. But when we come to deal with God in Christ, we come to have heavenly blessings, blessings beyond the power of nature, yea, beyond all those blessings that nature can convey, beyond all the blessings that the creature can hold. They have the blessing from God immediately by the mediation of Christ.

They enjoy God in Christ, and so come to enjoy God in a heavenly, supernatural way. Oh, this is the way to have our conversations in heaven! And those Christians who are well acquainted with the gospel of Christ come to live far more heavenly lives than others who go on in a dull, heavy, natural kind of service. But the hearts of those who are not acquainted with this mystery lie low upon the earth, and do not know what it is to have their conversations in heaven

RULE 7. So the next rule, with which I must close all this, is this: exercise much the grace of faith. There is no way to get above the creature, and above nature, but by exercising the grace of faith. Many Christians think they must exercise love for God, and exercise sorrow for sin. The grace of repentance, mourning for sin, is good. You should do that, and you should exercise patience; but the great grace that is to be employed if you would attain a heavenly life is the exercise of faith. Make conscience to put forth that grace much, for it is by faith that we converse with God through Christ. Though Christ is the ladder, it is faith that carries up this ladder and brings us down again.

It's faith that makes the things of heaven real to the soul (Hebrews 11:1). It's faith that is the evidence of things not seen and the substance of things hoped for. By faith these things come to be real and substantial things, present things. Faith is that which gives a great excellency to all the things of heaven itself. Therefore live much by faith. Walk by faith and not by your senses, and then you shall be above the world and live in heaven, and, as the fruit of your faith, wait for the appearing of Jesus Christ.

"Our conversation is in heaven," said the apostle, "from whence we also look for the Savior, the Lord Jesus Christ." Where a man's conversation is, his expectations will be; and where the expectations are, there is a man's conversation. Now our conversation is in heaven, from where we look for Jesus Christ. It's not a notion. Do not think that when we speak of conversing in heaven we are pleasing our own fancies. No, we, by faith, look upon heaven as the most real thing in the world, for we expect the Lord Jesus Christ to appear before long in glory bodily. We shall see Him with these eyes, and He shall change our vile bodies and make them like His glorious body. We, by faith, look upon such glorious things to be real and at hand, and waiting for these things makes our conversation to be in heaven.

Our hearts and all are there because we expect these things will be made good to us quickly. Christians, exercise your faith in this, in Jesus Christ. Put forth the fruit of faith by waiting for the appearing of Jesus Christ, when He shall come and appear in His glory. This will help make your conversations to be in heaven. Oh, what a blessed time that will be when Jesus Christ shall come from the heavens and appear to those who have been waiting for Him! It was a blessed thing to have Christ here personally, and to live with Him when He was upon the earth, even though it was in the state of His humiliation. When He shall come in His glory, how blessed that will be! He shall change our vile bodies so that they may be like His glorious body. Oh, this will keep the heart in expectation of Christ, for then that vile body of yours that is now a body of sin and death, of diseases, a body of weakness, and a lump of clay, shall be made like the glorious body of Jesus Christ, to shine more gloriously than the sun in the firmament!

This will be when Jesus Christ shall come with all His angels in glory. When all the glory of the creature shall be darkened with the glory of God and Jesus Christ, then the bodies of the saints shall shine gloriously before the face of God and Jesus Christ. Surely they shall be more glorious than the glory of the sun, for that, you know, will be darkened at the coming of Jesus Christ. The great glory of the Father, Jesus Christ, and the angels shall darken the glory of the sun, moon, and stars; but the glory of the bodies of the saints shall be so great that the glory of God, Jesus Christ, and the angels shall not darken their glory, but it shall appear with a very great luster. Now, if the glory of God and the angels could darken it, to what purpose is it that their bodies shall be like the glorious body of Jesus Christ?

If a candle were raised to have so much luster and beauty that it would shine even if you put it in the middle of the sun, it would be a strange kind of light, you would say. It shall be so with the bodies of the saints. Though they are put into the midst of the glory of God and His Son, yet their very bodies shall shine in beauty and luster there. If we believed this, and waited for it every day, how it would change us!

I have a diseased and lumpy body, and it hinders me in every duty of worship and service. Wandering and vain thoughts lodge in me now; but I'll wait for that time when Christ shall come in all His glory, and make my body to be like His glorious body, to make it able to look upon the face of God, to be able to be exercised in holy duties to all eternity without any weariness, without any intermission. So shall the bodies of saints be raised to that power. Their bodies shall be so strong that their bodies shall be exercised about the highest thing possible for a creature. Wait for this. I have many things here that trouble my mind and spirit, and hinder me in my converse with heaven. But, in a while, the time will come when I shall be delivered from all troubles here, when Christ shall appear with His mighty angels to be admired by His saints, when He shall come to take the saints to judge the world and shall set all the saints upon thrones to judge the world. The expectation of this time will raise the heart very much to be in heaven.

When I consider the glory that shall be on my soul, I should think this way: if this body of mine that is a lump of flesh shall be, by the almighty power of God, whereby He is able to subdue all things unto Himself, raised to that height of glory to be more glorious than the sun in the firmament, then to what height of glory shall my soul be raised! But not only my soul, but my grace, the divine nature that is in my soul, to what level shall that be raised?

The plants are capable of being raised to a higher excellency than stones, the rational creature to a higher excellency than a sensitive creature, the sensitive higher than the vegetative, and the supernatural creature to a higher excellency than the natural. Then raise your thoughts like this: my body shall be raised so high, what shall my soul be then? What shall my graces be that are in my soul? Oh, wait for this! It is only a little while before you shall be with God, for Him to be all in all to your soul enjoying full communion with Him. Exercise faith; wait for it; look for it every day. Consider that it is nearer and nearer; your salvation is nearer than when you first believed. God has a little work for you here, but, as soon as this is done, this shall be your condition: you shall see your Savior; your soul shall immediately be with Him and enjoy full communion with Him in glory, and your body, in a while, shall be raised and shall live forever with Him. You shall be where He is, and shall enjoy all that He has purchased with His blood. As much glory as the blood of Christ is worth, that is what you are capable of. The Scripture says that it shall be a weight of glory.

I am not fit here to bear a weight of glory. If the glory of heaven should shine upon me as much as it might, it would swallow me up. We read in Daniel 7 that, upon God's glory appearing to Daniel, he said, "I, Daniel, fainted, and was sick certain days." If God should open the heavens and dart some light from heaven to us as He could, alas, we should faint and be sick and die. No man can see God and live. No man can here enjoy that which God has prepared for His saints in heaven and live. Therefore, let us be content for a while to be as we are, and exercise your faith and hope in what shall be.

You shall be able to bear that weight of glory, and be able to stand before the face of God continually, to enjoy those things that eye has not seen, nor ear heard, nor can the mind of man conceive. Though a man has a spiritual eye, a spiritual ear, and a spiritual heart enlarged to supernatural things, they are things not only beyond the eye of sense, but the eye of reason. The eye of faith has not seen them fully, nor has the ear ever heard, nor have these things entered into a gracious heart. But those clusters we have of the land of Canaan show us that there is a glorious rest for His people. Now, by the exercise of your faith and hope, these things work upon your souls every day. It would be a mighty help to make your conversation to be in heaven. Where should my heart and thoughts, my life and conversation be but where I expect such things as these to be revealed very soon in the day of Jesus Christ, in His appointed time, which is at hand.

Of Walking With God

"And Enoch walked with God, and he was not,
for God took him."

<small>GENESIS 5:24</small>

CHAPTER ONE

The Text Opened

In this chapter we have the genealogy from Adam to Noah; and it's observable that God passes all over and says that Adam lived so long and begat sons, and so afterwards they lived and begat sons and daughters and then died. He only mentions them briefly until He comes to Enoch, and there God seems to make a stop. He not only tells you how long he lived, and that he begat sons and daughters and died, but He adds, "Enoch walked with God." The Holy Ghost spends three verses on Enoch. He tells you how long he lived, that he begat Methuselah, and that Enoch walked with God. In the 23rd verse He speaks of him again, and in the 24th verse Enoch walked with God again. It is as if the Lord should say, "Oh, my servant Enoch! I must not pass him by. He was an eminent, holy man in his generation. I must not pass by him without some special testimony." It is as if God should say, "Oh, he was the delight of My soul; he walked with Me." Enoch walked with God.

Enoch was a prophet in his time. He conversed much with God and God revealed much of His mind to him. We find in Jude 14 that the Holy Ghost mentions him again," Enoch also, the seventh from Adam, prophesied of these, saying. . . ." Enoch prophesied; he was a prophet. Where do we find Enoch's prophesies in all the Book of God? We have the prophesies of Isaiah, Jeremiah, and other prophets, but where is the prophesy of Enoch? Here the Holy Ghost says that Enoch prophesied saying, "Behold the Lord cometh with ten thousand of His saints."

Now for the prophecy that is mentioned by the Holy Ghost here in Jude, we do not have it set down in words fully; but we have something set down in a verse or two before my text. Enoch's prophecy is in the name of his son, Methuselah. The prophecy of which the Holy Ghost speaks in the Epistle of Jude is in the name of his son, Methuselah, for Methuselah signifies this much; he died and then came the flood. That's the significance of the name Methuselah. So that Enoch prophesied many hundreds of years before the flood came.

God's dealings with people in those times were only a type of His dealing with men in later times. The Lord would send forth a flood against all wicked and ungodly men in due time to destroy them. Methuselah died, and then came the sending of the flood. The flood came in the very last year of Methuselah, and it's observable that this Methuselah lived longer than any man has lived since the world began. All the days of Methuselah were nine hundred and sixty nine years and then he died. This may be one reason for the lengthening of his life, that he might fulfill the prophesy of Enoch; for Enoch prophesied that the flood should come when he died. Now because God had work to bring about and to defer the flood for a while, Methuselah lived as long as he did.

God lengthens or shortens men's lives according to the work He has to do, according to the use He has for them. But thus much for Enoch, and the person he was.

Enoch walked with God. This phrase, walking with God, sometimes signifies some special ministration before the Lord, as it does in 1 Samuel 2:30 and 35: "Wherefore the Lord God of Israel saith, 'I said indeed that thy house, and the house of thy father should walk before Me forever." And in the 35th verse, "I will raise Me up a faithful priest that shall do according to that which is in My heart, and in My mind, and I will build him a sure house, and he shall *walk* before Mine anointed forever," that is, for a special and holy ministration; so it is taken sometimes.

But here we are to understand it more largely (though it's true, Enoch was a prophet, and he might be said to walk with God in regard of the special ministration of the prophetic office that he had) for walking with God in ways of righteousness and holiness. So that walking with God, as it is said of Noah in Genesis 6:9, was his great-grandchild: "These are the generations of Noah. Noah was a just man and perfect in his generation, and Noah walked with God." That was his great-grandchild (there is no question that hearing of his fathers walking with God was a great motivation to move him to do likewise), and his walking with God is described as being righteous, in being perfect with God. The Septuagint translates "walk with God" by the words "he pleased God." It's observable that the Holy Ghost, in mentioning Enoch in the New Testament, follows the Septuagint translation in Hebrews 11. There you find that Enoch is mentioned among the believers: "By faith, Enoch was translated that he should not see death, and was not found, because God had translated him."

Before his translation he had this testimony: he pleased God. The words that Genesis translates "he walked with God", Hebrews renders, "he pleased God." Indeed, it is apparent that he walked in the ways in which God was delighted and pleased.

"He pleased God." The Chaldeans translate it, "he walked

in the fear of God." And so some interpreters, quoting the *Jerusalemie Targum*, say that he served or labored in the truth before the Lord. One thing further to be noted is that it is said that Enoch walked with God after he begat Methuselah. Some now think that Enoch was a wicked man before he begat Methuselah. In the sixty-five years prior to this there is no mention of his walking with God, but Enoch lived sixty-five years and begat Methuselah, and he walked with God after he begat Methuselah. That is no sufficient ground to conclude that he did not walk with God before, however. It might rather be better to note the constancy of his walking with God, that he continued in the constant course of his life walking with God. I need to speak no further in explaining this first part of Enoch's walking with God. The point of doctrine from it follows.

CHAPTER TWO

The Doctrines Raised from the Text

It is the great excellency and commendation of a godly man to walk with God. It is the highest testimony that can be given of a man that he walks with God. Walking with God is a high excellency, and whoever has this testimony has the highest testimony that can be given to a man in this world, "he walks with God." Therefore it is observable that God mentions Enoch twice, as if He loved to mention His poor creatures walking with Him, as in the 22nd verse: "And Enoch walked with God." Then again in the 24th verse: "And Enoch walked with God." Oh! It is as if God should say, "This is that which is the delight of My soul indeed!" Yea, and that is observable in the testimony of Noah in Genesis 6:9. (Perhaps in reading it you may not observe that which I shall open to you now.) He said, "Noah was a just man, perfect in his generation, and Noah walked with God." He does not say that Noah was a just man and walked with God, but note that He repeats Noah twice. Noah was a just man and perfect in his generations, and Noah walked with God. It is as if He should say, "This is the blessed man who lived in a wicked generation; and though that generation was sinful and wicked, he kept close to God. Noah was just and perfect. Noah walked with God. Oh, I take delight in this Noah! Consider My servant Noah!" Noah was thus, and Noah walked with God.

There is a great emphasis in doubling his name; and there can be no reason given for it, for the meaning would be clear without it. It is as if He should say, "Noah was a just man and perfect in his generation, and walked with God." Oh, 'tis the excellency of a man to walk with God, and for God Himself to acknowledge a man and to say that he walks with Him! Men may live in a practice of the duties of religion, eternal duties, and go very far in that way and yet be strangers to God, never knowing what it is to walk with God. They may have byways of their own in which their hearts walk.

Many in their external profession seem to be moved one way, but secretly their hearts turn another way. They do not walk with God all the while. They pray, read, hear sermons, and make great professions, so that men might think they walked with God, but it is not so. A ship may be bound to a port, and the ship and the sails blow that way, yet while the ship is going east a man may walk up and down the ship westward. So in profession, a man may seem to be carried eastward, yet his private walks may be another way, to his own ends, to his own designs. The honor of a man is when God Himself shall acknowledge him, as if God should say concerning Enoch, "I, who am a God, who is the Seer and Searcher of all men's hearts, observe the ways of My servant Enoch. I see him not only in the outward profession of godliness, but in the secret of his soul he walks with Me. He has no byways at all, but keeps himself close with Me and walks with Me continually." Enoch walked with God.

This phrase, "walking with God," is expressed in Scripture in various other phrases that have the same meaning as walking before God. "The Lord before whom I walk," said Abraham.

And so God bade Abraham, "Walk before Me and be upright." Psalm 116:9: "I will walk before the Lord in the land of the living." Hezekiah said, "Remember how I have walked before Thee."

Sometimes the same thing is expressed by walking *after* the Lord, as in Deuteronomy 13:4: "Ye shall walk after the Lord." As a child walks after his father, though he is always a step behind, he is still said to be walking with him. Sometimes this phrase is used, "walking in the name of the Lord." Micah 4:5: "We will walk in the name of the Lord our God." There is also "walking in the spirit of God," as in Galatians 5:16. So walking with God is also expressed by:

- Walking before God
- Walking after God
- Walking in the name of God
- Walking in the Spirit of God

They all have the same meaning. But for the opening of the point, there are these four things that I intend to handle.

First, what it is to walk with God, or to describe the work of God in bringing the soul to walk with Him, and the way of the soul in walking with God.

Second, to show you the excellency that there is in this walking with God, what a blessed thing it is for a Christian to walk with God.

Third, give you some evidences of a man's walking with God.

Fourth, to give unto you some rules as to how you may come to walk with God, to have your lives so that you may have this testimony from God Himself, that you walk with Him.

CHAPTER THREE

How the Soul Is Brought to Walk with God

Everyone, by nature, goes astray from God. In Psalm 58:3 it is said of the wicked that they are estranged from the womb. They go astray as soon as they are born, speaking lies. That's one of the first things wherein wickedness appears in children. And it is from the very womb that they go astray, before they can speak. It is natural for the wicked to go astray from God as soon as they have any being. The way men naturally walk is the way of death; it's the way of their own hearts, of their own counsels. It's the common course of this world; it is the walk of the flesh.

God works, though, to bring the soul to walk with Him. First, He causes the soul to stop walking the way men naturally walk. Those whom the Lord has left for a while in the way of nature, those who walk in the way of death, the Lord is pleased to come to them by some mighty work of His to make them stop by considering, "Where am I? What's my way? Where am I going? Is the way I am in like the way that suits an immortal soul? Is the way likely to end well in which I am walking?"

It causes the soul to stop and think about where it is and where it is going. It fears that it is in a way that is likely to miscarry, so that it dares not proceed further in the way it has been walking all this time. Though that way is never so pleasant, though it is never so suitable to the flesh, the Lord forbid that I should go on in that way. This stop of the soul is like that which happened to Saul. When he was about to die, a light shone round him and caused him to stop so that he could go no further.

Second, the Lord manifests to the soul the way of life and what it is. Isaiah 30:21: "And thine ears shall hear a word behind thee saying, 'This is the way, walk ye in it.' " Oh, how many there are who can tell this by experience, that they have been walking in the ways of death, of eternal misery, and who have blessed themselves in those ways! But there was a blessed time when God caused them to hear a voice, as it were, behind them saying, "This is the way, walk in it. You are out of the way of life, but here's the way of life. If you would not perish eternally, here's the way; walk in this way." It is a secret voice that the Lord causes to be heard in the soul, but it is a powerful voice.

Perhaps you have come to the Word and have heard what the way of life is, but yet that has never turned your heart. But when God would have the soul to come in to walk with Him He causes the soul to hear a voice in secret, powerfully saying, "Oh, this is the way! O you poor soul, that is wandering away from the way of life and is going in the way of eternal death, come in, come in! There's another way. This is the way, walk in it!" And so the Lord gives a mighty turn to the soul by that secret voice.

Third, the Lord makes peace between Himself and a sinner. He reveals the doctrine of reconciliation. When a sinner first comes to have his eyes enlightened, comes to know himself and to know God, certainly God cannot at first appear to be anything but terrible to a sinner who has formerly walked in the ways of death. Though he sees his way to be dangerous and another way to be good, God is terrible to him. And how can those two walk together who are not at peace? Amos 3:3: "How can two walk together except they be agreed?" There is a natural enmity between man and God. Every man in the world is naturally an enemy to God; and can there be two walking together unless they agree?

You who are going on in the ways of enmity with God, surely you are strangers to this way of walking with God. Can you walk with God before you are in harmony? No soul can have this testimony given of it, that he walked with God, but a soul that is reconciled to Him. God manifests that in some measure to the soul before it's able to walk with Him as Enoch did. Enoch came to walk with God by this, for the Holy Ghost, in Hebrews 11, said that it was by faith that he did it, and that without faith it's impossible to please God. That's the same as saying that without faith it's impossible to walk with God. The Holy Ghost means the same thing when the apostle said that he walked by faith, and without faith it is impossible to please God. Therefore, there must be a work of faith to bring the soul to be reconciled; and there must be an agreement between the soul and God before it can walk with Him.

Fourth, though peace is made so that God does not appear as an enemy against the soul, there may be some strangeness still after peace is made. There was peace made between David and Absalom. David was pacified towards him, yet he would not see his face for a while. He would have been gone from his presence. There would not be that conversation with him in the familiar way that a child has with his father for a while. So, though peace is made, there is required a further work of God for the soul's walking with Him, that is, that God should offer Himself in loveliness and fullness of mercy, sweetness and delightfulness unto the soul so that there may be a familiarity between the soul and God. It's one thing for me to know that

God is not my enemy, that He does not intend wrath and misery against me; but it is another thing for the soul to apprehend the sweet, delightful countenance of God, and the embracements in the arms of His mercy, and those condescensions of God, that He is willing to come and deal with us as a friend in a familiar way.

The Lord is pleased to manifest Himself to the soul in the sweetness of His love and His delight. Not only is it, "You are that soul that shall not be damned, but shall be eternally saved," but, "You are the soul that My soul delights in; you are one whom I take as My friend, and who I love to deal with in all sweetness, and to bring into familiarity with Myself." This is that which is manifested to the soul to bring it to this walking with God that the Holy Ghost here speaks of concerning Enoch.

Fifth, the Lord is pleased to send His Holy Spirit to guide the soul to Himself, and to guide it in walking with Himself. In Romans 8 it is said, "All that are the sons of God are led by the Spirit of God." When a father walks with his child, he gives him his hand and leads the child along beside himself. When anyone comes to be a child of God, God puts forth His hand and leads him, and so they walk together. Have you not seen a father and child walking in the garden, and the father puts forth his finger and the child takes hold of it and walks beside him? Even so, the Lord puts forth His Spirit into a gracious soul, and God and the soul walk together, being led by the Spirit of God.

In Isaiah 35:8–9, you see that the Lord speaks of the way of His redeemed ones: "And a highway shall be there, and a way, and it shall be called the way of holiness. The unclean shall not pass over it, but it shall be for those; the wayfaring men, though fools, shall not err therein." Though they are very weak and fools, yet they shall not err therein. No lion shall be there, nor shall any ravenous beast go there. The redeemed shall walk there; that's their privilege. This way of walking up unto the land of Canaan from their captivity typifies the walk of the soul with the Lord.

Sixth, this if further done by God for the soul's walking with God: Christ the Son of God takes the soul and brings it unto God the Father as the Spirit leads. The Lord Jesus Christ brings the soul unto the Father to render God and the soul familiar together. Ephesians 2:18: "Through Him we have an access by one Spirit unto the Father." We have access through Him. He brings us to the Father; we have access through Jesus Christ.

Suppose a prince should take a traitor who has been pardoned by his father, the king. The king has been pacified and the traitor has his pardon. The prince takes the traitor by the hand and says, "Come, I'll bring you to my father; and I will walk along with you to my father." In the same way, no one who has ever been a sinner can walk with God unless Christ walks together with him. Christ walks along with him, and God is rendered more sweet, amiable, and lovely. Why? Because Christ has him by one hand and God the Father has him by the other hand. And so the soul walks in this blessed walk between the hands of God the Father and the Son, and the Holy Ghost leads and guides him, too.

CHAPTER FOUR

What Walking With God Is

QUESTION. When the soul is brought to God, and by these means enabled to walk with Him, then what's the way of the soul in walking with God?

ANSWER. I shall answer in these nine particulars:

1. Walking with God causes the soul to eye God. The soul, having come to God, eyes God in all the ways of God; it sets God before it. Enoch walked with God. That is, Enoch, in the ways of his life, set God before Him and eyed God in his ways. First, he beheld the infinite beauty that is in God. Second, he saw God is the Fountain of all good to the soul. Third, the soul apprehends God as infinitely worthy of all honor. These three things cause the eye to be upon God continually.

The Lord has infinite excellency and beauty in Him. The Lord is the Fountain of all good to me. The Lord is infinitely worthy of all honor and service; and a soul walking with God eyes God thus continually. Psalm 26:3: "For Thy loving kindness is before mine eyes, and I have walked in Thy truth." O Lord! I see Thee as amiable, lovely, and gracious, and the Fountain of all good. Lord, I have walked in Thy truth, setting God before Me. So Psalm 16:8: "I have set the Lord always before me that I might not fall!"

A soul that walks with God scarcely eyes anything but God, as the little child who walks with his father looks up to the father. Every soul that walks with God has his eye upon Him, for there is no object so lovely to draw the soul as God Himself. Whereas wicked men do not find God to be such a lovely object, they see no such excellency in Him; and therefore, rather, they turn their eyes away from Him and look another way. Psalm 86:14: "They do not set God before them." Men who walk according to the lusts of their own hearts, in their wicked, sinful ways, do not have the Lord in all their thoughts, as in Psalm 10. That's the first thing in the way of the soul's walking with God: he eyes God and sets God before him.

2. Walking with God causes a man to carry himself as in God's presence. The soul behaves itself as if in God's presence. I see myself in God's presence, and my eye is upon God. Oh, then, let me look to myself, so that the carriage of my soul is suitable to one who is in the presence of so holy, so great, so glorious and blessed a God as the Lord is! 2 Corinthians 2:17: "As of God in the sight of God speak we in Christ," said the apostle. When we come to do anything, we do it as of God in the sight of God, knowing that we are always before God. Augustine, speaking about Noah's walking with God, used this expression, "Noah walked with God, that is, he always had God present before his eyes, walking so holily; and so he reverenced God."

This is to walk in the fear of God, when the soul, upon the apprehension of God's presence, shall labor to compose itself as is appropriate to the presence before whom it is. This indeed is the walk in which you shall find the saints of God all the day long. Would you know where to find a saint? You may know his walk; all the day long you shall find him walking in the fear of the Lord. Proverbs 23:17: "Let not thy heart envy sinners, but be thou in the fear of the Lord all the day long." He does not say, "Fear the Lord all the day long," but rather, "Be in the fear of the Lord all the day long." Oh, the walk of a Christian should be so from morning to night, to walk in the fear of the Lord. Nothing in this world should put him out of this walk. No temptations should call him out of it, but he should be in the fear of the Lord all the day long. This is the walk of a Christian, when he labors to behave himself as is suitable to being in the presence of God.

3. Walking with God is when we make God's will the rule of our will. The soul does what God does. What's the way of God but the way of holiness and righteousness, when the soul makes the will of God to be its own rule? I will not act on my own will. I will not act on anything but the will of God. What is it that God wills? Then I will the same thing. The soul walks the way God walks when it suits itself with God, when it sets the Lord as an example before it. The Scripture says, "Be ye holy as your heavenly Father is holy." I see the holy and righteous ways of God, and I labor as a dear child to follow Him and to go in the very same steps that God does. How does God carry Himself in business? I will labor to carry things as God does so that my life shall hold forth a resemblance of God Himself. This is to walk with God, to do as God does, to imitate God.

4. Walking with God is when a soul has the same ends that God has. We are not only to do the same thing, to make the will of God to be the rule, but to have the same ends that God has. What's the end that God has in all His ways? Surely, it is that His blessed name may be magnified, that His glory may be set forth. Then that shall be the great design of my life. My soul shall aim at that as the highest end of all things, and all things shall be subordinate to the glory and honor of God. It is that

at which God aims, and therefore it is that at which I will aim. Thus the soul goes along with God.

A man may be said to go along with another man when they both aim at the same ends. Oh, this is a blessed thing, indeed! We shall speak to that hereafter, but the very opening shows much of the excellency of it. I beseech you, as you go along examine your own hearts. See whether, by the very mentioning of these things, you are not strangers to God. Examine by the workings of God in bringing your souls to walk with Him, or otherwise by the way of the soul in eyeing God, in behaving itself as in the presence of God, in making the will of God to be its rule, and in aiming at the design that God does.

5. Walking with God is observing the administrations of God, and suiting the soul to them. God sometimes seems to work in one way, sometimes in another way. The soul that walks with God observes the various ways and administrations of God in the world and labors to suit its heart to them. Sometimes the Lord is in a way of judgments, heavy and dreadful afflictions in the world, sometimes against His own saints and people. Then let me suit my heart according to this. "O Lord! We will wait upon Thee in the ways of Thy judgments," said the church in Isaiah. Are we under God's way of judgments, in a way of affliction? Lord, we will suit ourselves to honor Thee according to that way. We will labor to exercise those graces that are suitable to those ways of Thine.

Lord, art Thou in a way of mercy? We will suit ourselves accordingly, and labor to exercise those graces that are suitable to Thy ways. Art Thou in a way of affliction in my family, or in a way of mercy? I will labor, Lord, to exercise those graces that are suitable to Thy ways. This is to walk with God. If I am walking with a man and he turns this way, then I go with him; and if he turns the other way, then I suit myself to go that way with him. So, though the ways of God are never so varied, yet the soul that walks with God is suitable to the ways of God.

This is a great art, a great mystery, to suit a man's self to these varied administrations of God in the world. You shall have some who, if God goes the way of mercy, oh, they can bless and praise God. They think that this is to walk with God; but if God turns His back on them and takes away their earthly comfort, and so comes in a way of affliction, how do they suit themselves to God's ways then? When God was in a way of mercy, their exercise was in joy and thankfulness, speaking good of His name. But now that the Lord is in a way of affliction, do I exercise faith in God? Do I exercise patience? Do I exercise Christian wisdom, to know what good I can get out of the hand of God? Whatever courses God takes, a Christian has several graces to exercise in several conditions. The soul can exercise joy and thanksgiving, and speaking good of His name, and not just while God is in a smooth path. To walk with God is to have the soul suit itself to God, according to His various administrations.

6. Walking with God is to have a holy dependence upon God in all His ways.

First, the soul depends upon God for direction. "Oh, lead me in the way of truth." A Christian looks to God and depends on Him in the constant course of his life, depends upon Him for direction. "O Lord! Teach me Thy way, Lord; lead me in the way of everlasting life, Lord. Send forth Thy light and Thy truth to guide me. Thou shalt be my Guide even unto death." The soul dares not go one step further than it sees God going before it; and, therefore, it says, "Lord, lead me, guide me."

I beseech you to examine as you go along. Can you say that in the course of your lives you find that you walk in a holy dependence on God for guidance and direction in every step?

Whatever you meddle with, still your walk is in a holy dependence upon God for direction in your business; and according as the business is of greater or lesser consequence, the heart works more after God for guidance and direction for that business. The men of the world are afraid that God might lead them into hard paths, into troublesome ways, and therefore they are shy of God's guidance. This is the way of wicked hearts; they are shy of the guidance and direction of God. But a gracious heart says, "Let God lead me, and let the way be what it will be." The wicked are guided by their own thoughts, by their own counsels, by the examples of other men, what is most suitable to their own ends. But the way of the saints is this: "Lord, guide me."

Second, their holy dependence upon God is for protection, to protect them in what they do. Lord, I am in the way into which Thou hast guided me. I may meet with much trouble and affliction; but, Lord, protect me, defend me in this way of Thine. If the child, walking with his father, hears any noise that scares him, he immediately looks up to his father and depends on his father to protect him. So, when a child of God shall, in all his ways, walk in a holy dependence upon God for protection, this is to walk with God.

Third, the soul depends upon God for assistance in anything it undertakes. Lord, this is the work that Thou hast called me to. Oh, let me have strength from Thee in this work. I can do nothing without Thee, Lord; and let me have assistance from Thee. The wicked make flesh their arm; and therefore there's a curse pronounced against them, as in Jeremiah 17:5. They are strangers to any such work as this, of dependence upon God for assistance. Now and then they will say that God must help them, and that they can do nothing without God. Aye, but to have a holy, gracious frame of spirit, to walk in a holy dependence upon God for assistance in every business, this is far from the wicked and ungodly.

Fourth, the soul walks in a holy dependence upon God for a blessing upon all it does. "Walk before Me and be upright. I am your exceeding great reward." It is as if God should say to Abraham, "Walk in dependence upon Me. I am your reward. Though you have little encouragement in the world, yet look to Me for your reward." Lord, I depend upon Thee for a blessing; and, however things seem to go, still, Lord, I look up to Thee to bring all to a good issue." Here is a soul walking with God, when the soul turns from men and the world and does not mind so much what encouragement it has from the world, but looks up to God.

7. Walking with God makes a man free and ready in the ways of God. One who walks with God in all His ways of holiness and obedience has a free heart within him; he comes off readily to every good work. He is not hauled and pulled to God, but he walks with Him. There is a great deal of difference between one who is dragged (as you would drag a prisoner who had no mind to go that way) and one who walks up and down with delight and pleasure with you. It is not enough to walk with God, to be in the way that God would have you be, or to do the things that God would have you do, unless our hearts come off freely in the ways of obedience, unless you choose the ways of holiness as the ways that are most suitable to you. This is walking with God.

In Psalm 119:45, David said, "I will walk at liberty, for I seek Thy precepts." It's a notable Scripture. The men of the world think that there is no walking at liberty except to satisfy their desires to the uttermost, to walk after their lusts, which is the Scripture phrase. "No," said David, "my liberty is this: I seek Thy precepts." A carnal heart thinks it is the greatest bondage in the world to seek the precepts of God and to conform to

God's precepts. That is bondage, to walk according to rules! No, said David, I'll walk at liberty, for I seek Thy precepts." It's an excellent argument of grace in the heart to account the precepts of God to be the greatest liberty to the soul.

When I am in the ways of sin I am in the ways of bondage, I am a slave to Satan, but when I seek God's precepts I am at liberty. When a man is walking up and down in the fields he is at liberty. So when the soul is walking with God it is at liberty; but when the soul is walking without God it is in a dungeon, a prison. But when it walks with God it is at liberty; it comes off freely in all the ways of obedience.

8. Walking with God consists in communion with God. Walking with God consists in the conversation and communion that the soul has with Him in holy duties. There are the special walks of the soul with God, and of God, with the soul in the duties of holy worship. In Leviticus 18:4, the Lord said, "Ye shall do My judgments and keep Mine ordinances, to WALK therein. I am the Lord your God." You must walk in God's ordinances. The ordinances of God are the walks of a gracious soul; and there the soul meets with God. Leviticus 26:11-12 is a notable Scripture to show that in God's ordinances the soul meets with God: "And I will set My tabernacle amongst you, and My soul shall not abhor you, that is, shall delight in you, and I will *walk* among you, and will be your God, and ye shall be My people."

"I will set My tabernacle amongst you." What's that? "That is My ordinances. You shall enjoy My ordinances; you shall have the duties of My worship, and I will walk among you."

God walks among us when we walk in His ordinances. So you see in Leviticus 18 that God said, "You shall walk in My ordinances." The ordinances are the godly man's walk, and in Leviticus 26 the ordinances are God's walk—so we see that they walk the same way. There God and a gracious heart meet together. The candlesticks that we read of in Revelation 1:13 are the churches enjoying ordinances. "In the midst of the seven golden candlesticks was one like unto the Son of Man, clothed with a garment down to the feet, and girded about the paps with a golden girdle." The Lord Jesus Christ is in the midst of the candlesticks, that is, in the midst of the churches. Where there are ordinances of God, there He is. If you would walk with Him, you must find Him there. In Psalm 68:24, you may see what is the way of a gracious heart in walking with God: "They have seen Thy goings, O God, even the going of my God, my King." Where? "In the sanctuary."

If you would walk with another man you must know where his destination is, observe where he usually walks, and go there. "They have seen Thy going, O God, even the goings of my God, my King, in the sanctuary." There are the goings of God. If you would meet with God and walk with Him, it must be in the sanctuary; it must be in His ordinances. In Song of Solomon 7:5, it is said that the King (speaking of Christ) is held in the galleries. Now, what is that but in the ordinances? That is, as it were, the galleries of the great King of heaven and earth. You know that princes and great men have their sumptuous galleries where they walk, and only their chief favorites are permitted to walk there. "The King is held in his galleries," that is, when Jesus Christ is in communion with His saints in His ordinances, in the duties of worship.

Oh, 'tis the most pleasant galleries, to walk in what He has! It's as pleasant a gallery as He has in heaven itself. Oh, He loves to be there; the King is held there. Oh, a gracious heart has many a sweet and comfortable turn in these galleries, that is, in the ordinances and duties of worship in walking with Jesus Christ!

When the soul is exercised in the ordinances it has conversed with Christ; it harkens to what Christ says, and Christ harkens to what such a soul says. The soul knows the voice of Christ. "It is the voice of my beloved," said the spouse (Song of Solomon 5:2). It knows that the voice of Christ is when they walk together in the ordinances. Christ speaks to the soul, and the soul knows His voice. And the soul speaks again to Jesus Christ; there is a blessed conversation between them. Christ lets Himself into the heart and the heart opens itself to Christ. Oh, the communion that a gracious heart has with Jesus Christ is unspeakable! Only those who are acquainted with it understand the meaning of conversing with God.

It is with many as it was with Adam, that when God came to walk in the garden, we read that he hid in the bush. The ordinances and duties of worship are as paradise, Eden; and God comes many times to walk with us, and would have communion and conversation with us. Yet how many times do many of His servants hide in the bush? They have walked loosely, and contracted some guilt upon their spirits, and so the presence of God is terrible to them. And the more the voice of God and the presence of God are in an ordinance, the more they are afraid because of guilt. They are entangled in the bush when they should be conversing with God.

Oh, the difference there is between some Christians and others in exercising themselves in the duties of worship! Oh, what sweet and blessed terms and communion between God and their souls some have when they are worshipping God! Others, though they have some good in them, are entangled in the briars of the world; and, though God is in the midst of His ordinances, they have no conversation, no communion at all with Him.

9. Walking with God causes the soul to follow God more as He reveals Himself. The soul that walks with God, as God

reveals Himself unto it more and more, follows God more and more and still seeks to glorify God more and more. That's walking! There is a progress in the ways of godliness where there is a walking. When the soul is first led by the hand of Jesus Christ to God and walks with Him, 'tis sweet and comfortable! But still, as God reveals Himself more and more to the soul, the soul still grows up in godliness more and more, and still is more holy and more gracious, and honors God more in the life than it had formerly done. It gets nearer and nearer to heaven every day; this is to walk with God.

There is a notable Scripture in Psalm 63:8, where David says, "My soul follows hard after Thee, O Lord. Thy right hand upholdeth me." A poor child who walks with his father may be weak and cannot go as fast as he desires, but the father puts forth his hand, and takes hold of him, and so upholds and strengthens the child, and the child follows hard after the father. So it is here. "O Lord, Thy right hand upholds me. If it did not uphold me, I could not walk. But Thy right hand upholds me, and then my soul follows hard after Thee, and so increases in godliness more and more."

"I will praise Thee more and more," said David, speaking of the honor that he desired to give to God in his way. He professed he would still add to the praise of God, and praise Him more and more. These are the principal things wherein walking with God consists.

Now, to all these, consider what we have mentioned all along, that all these are in a constant course of a man's life. Some other men, who do not know what it is to walk with God, may, perhaps, come and walk a step or two in God's ways; but they quickly turn out again and find them tedious and irksome. But the heart that walks with God does all that I have named. That is, he eyes God in all his ways, behaves itself as if in the presence of God, walks in the same way God does, and observes God's designs. All this is the constant course of his life.

It is true that through the violence of some temptation there may be a stray step, or there may be, perhaps, a fall along the way; but still the heart is God-ward and still is towards God. It gets up again and walks again in the way. It does not merely go a step in the way of God as some carnal men do. Sometimes, when God's hand is upon them, or upon the hearing of some sermon, their hearts are a little touched and they seem to be a little forward; but take the constant course of their lives and it's the way of sin. But the constant course of the ways of the saints is the ways of God.

A swine may go through a fair meadow, but it would rather be in the dirt and mire; there it wallows. So it is with many wicked men. They will come and hear, pray, and do some good duties. They are like swine in a meadow. But when they come to those ways that may satisfy the lusts of the flesh, there they wallow; that's their proper place, and, therefore, they are far from walking with God. A beggar will, perhaps, follow a man a little way, as long as he has hopes of getting something from him; but if the man goes away from him, he will turn aside to another way; he will go no further with him. So it is with many men. Many professors seem to follow God, perhaps for comfort, and for something that they would have from Him; but if they cannot get what they want from God, then they turn aside.

This is the difference between a friend who walks with another because of the delight of communion, and a beggar who only goes along begging for a handout. The man who goes along begging does not regard the company of this man any further than his hopes of getting something from him. If he cannot have what he would have, or if he gets what he wants, he will turn aside from the man. But a friend who is walking with his friend is satisfied with the company of his friend, and the conversation he has with him while they walk. So he goes on in a constant way and walks where his friend is going. He is sorry that the walk is so short and still desires to converse with his friend.

So, I say, this is the difference in professors. There are some who have some touch of conscience, and they see that there is no way for them if they do not have mercy from God, that they must perish. Perhaps they will be seeking God, following God, and crying to God for mercy; but if they do not have comfort according to their expectations they will turn away from Him and seek comfort in other ways. But a gracious heart that is indeed turned to God not only seeks God for mercy for itself, so that it might be delivered from misery, but it sees an excellency in God, and finds sweetness in conversation and communion with God, and loves the presence of God. This is the ground of the constancy of his heart in the ways of holiness, because it loves the presence of God so much and communion with God. It is for God Himself that the soul is in those ways; and such a one will hold out in the ways of God.

Indeed, one who merely serves God in a servile way, and seeks himself in seeking God, will be ready to turn aside; but where the soul walks with God out of a sense of communion, sweetness, and the good that there is in communion with God, such a man goes on in a constant way to the end and is not tired in the ways of God as others are. You know, if you are walking from place to place and have good company with you, you are not weary; you count the journey as nothing. Why? Because you have good company, and especially if you have good conversation all along, too. So it is with Christians. Oh, the ways of God come to be very easy to them upon this ground, and so they hold out.

CHAPTER FIVE

Twelve Distinct Excellencies of Walking With God

The next thing is the excellency that there is in walking with God. There are twelve distinct excellencies:

1. There is an excellency in walking with God, if only that it makes the ways of God easy. How easy are all the ways of God to the soul that knows what this means (walking with God), who has God in his company continually. Oh, the ease that is in the ways of God! It's that which is worth a world; and men and women who have convinced consciences and dare not willfully go out of God's ways, but are always drooping and finding them grievous and tedious, are in a grievous and sad condition. But it is because they have no communion with God in them. David said, "When I am awake, I am always with Thee." The very nights are pleasant to them. When they awake, they are still with God.

Many men and women cannot lie alone. Some wake during the night and cannot sleep if they have no company with them; the nights are tedious. But, if they cannot sleep and wake to find someone with them, the nights are not so tedious to them. "When I awake I am ever with Thee," said David concerning God.

2. Walking with God is most honorable. Oh, 'tis an honorable thing to walk with God! We know that attending on kings and princes is honorable. The maids of honor that attend upon a queen have a great honor, attending upon a king, upon noble men. But now not only attendance, but free conversation with princes, that's more than mere attendance—to walk with an Emperor as a friend, up and down in his galleries, in his gardens, in his orchards. So it is with the saints. Abraham is called God's friend. "You are not My servants, but My friends," said Christ. God admits the soul to come as a friend and to have conversation with Him. Oh, this is honorable!

Those who were in the presence of Solomon, servants who waited on his table, were accounted blessed. How much more to sit at his table, to see the order of Solomon's table? Then, to always be with God, to walk with Him, what a blessed and honorable thing this is! It is the honor of the angels themselves that they see the face of God. The angels in heaven behold the face of God. What honor is it then for Christians to always be walking with God? Honor! 'Tis that which is the great honor and happiness of the church, when she shall be in her glory. Mark how Christ expresses Himself in Revelation 3:4: "Thou hast a few names even in Sardis, which have not defiled their garments." What's promised to them? "And they shall walk with Me in white, for they are worthy." A glory shall be put upon them and they shall walk with Me, for they are worthy. Walking with Christ is the greatest honor that Christ could put on them. So, in Revelation 14:4, it is said of those who stood upon Mount Zion with the Lamb, having harps in their hands and singing a new song: "These are they which were not defiled with women, for they are virgins; these are they which follow the Lamb where ever He goes, these were redeemed from among men, being the first fruit unto God and the Lamb." They follow the Lamb wherever He goes; this is the honor that is put upon them. Oh, walking with God is most honorable!

3. The excellency of walking with God consists in the blessed satisfaction that the soul must have in walking with Him. To walk with life itself, with glory, with happiness, and to do it constantly must satisfy the soul. This must, I say, bring inconceivable satisfaction and peace to the soul walking with Him. You know what Philip said, "Show us the Father and it sufficeth us." What? It would suffice Philip to see God? Then how much more not only to see Him, but to walk and continually be with Him!

People will run to see a great man; but to be admitted into the same room, and to walk with him is far more. Exodus 33:14: "And He said, My presence shall go with thee, and I will give thee rest." God promised Moses that His presence would be with him. Oh, the rest that the soul has by the presence of God! Oh, the joy that there must be to the heart that walks with God! Psalm 36:8–9: "They shall be abundantly satisfied with the fatness of Thy house, and Thou shalt make them drink of the rivers of Thy pleasures; for with Thee is the fountain of life: In Thy light shall we see light."

Certainly where God walks there is a glorious light round about. Such a soul never walks in darkness; the light of God shines about it. We read of those who walked with Christ to Emmaus that their hearts burned within them. Certainly the hearts of saints who walk with God must be filled with the influences from God that make their hearts glow within them while they are walking with Him. In Psalm 89:15-16, you have a notable Scripture about the satisfaction of the soul who walks with God: "Blessed are the people that know the joyful sound: they shall walk, O Lord, in the light of Thy countenance, In Thy name shall they rejoice all the day, and in Thy righteousness shall they be exalted."

Those who walk with God walk in the light of God's countenance, and in God's name they shall rejoice all the day, and in His righteousness they shall be exalted. Oh, what a blessed thing it is to walk with God! That noble Marques Galiatius, who was of a great birth in Italy, forsook all his honors and all his friends and came to Geneva. He said, at a time when he felt the sweetness of his conversation with God, "Cursed be that man who accounts all the gold and silver in the world worth one day's enjoyment of communion with Jesus Christ." He had a great deal of gold and silver; he had the Pope for a close relative; he had great possessions and relatives; and he left it all to come to Geneva, to profess the truth there. He found all recompensed in communion with Christ; and his heart was so full of it that he even cursed those who accounted all the gold and silver in the world to be worth the enjoyment of one hour's communion with Christ. Oh, an hour's walking with Christ is more than all the world!

I appeal to those souls who have been acquainted with this. Would you have lost an hour of conversing with God for all the world? What would you take for the enjoyment of such an hour as this? Oh, a gracious heart would not take a thousand thousands of worlds for hours of enjoying sweet communion with God in walking with Him. Oh, there's a infinite sweetness in walking with God! There's a great deal of good to be had in walking with the saints.

I have told you before of Dr. Taylor, the martyr. When he came to prison, he rejoiced that he was put in prison to meet with that angel of God, John Bradford. Now, if it is comfortable to have communion with the saints, even though they are in prison, how sweet is it to have communion with God in walking with Him!

I remember reading of a king who, beholding Plato walking up and down with another philosopher, cried out, "O life! This is life and true happiness; yonder is true happiness." He did not look on his kingdom as affording life to him. His kingdom could not give him the happiness that he believed Plato and the other philosopher had in conversing with each other about philosophy. It is as if he should say, " 'Tis not the kings of the earth that live the happy lives, but these philosophers that walk and converse thus with one another." Oh, then, what life and happiness it is for the soul to walk up and down with God, to converse with God Himself! Though you walk in the valley of Bacha, though you walk in the shadow of death in respect of outward afflictions, yet walking with God is that which will shine upon you, and will sweeten your heart even when you are walking in the valley of Bacha and the valley of death.

In Revelation 7, see how Jesus Christ leads the soul in walking with Him: "The Lamb which is in the midst of the throne shall feed them, and shall lead them unto living fountains of waters, and God shall wipe away all tears from their eyes." Thus, when you walk with Jesus Christ, He leads you to the living fountains of waters that comfort you. The comforts that you had in the world were just dirty puddles, but those comforts that you had in Christ, when you walked with Him, are the fountains of living waters. That's the third thing wherein the excellency of walking with God consists, in the abundance of soul satisfaction that the heart has in God.

4. The fourth excellency in walking with God is this: it is a special part of the covenant on our part that God makes with us, upon which the very blessing of the covenant in great part depends. Genesis 17 clearly shows this, where God comes to

make His covenant with Abraham, and to be a God to him and to his seed. What is it that God requires of Abraham now? "Walk before Me and be upright." It is as if God had said, "I am an all-sufficient God, and I am entering into covenant with you, to be a God to you and a God to your seed. Walk before Me and be upright." As if that were all that God looked at, that you should walk with Him and be upright; then you shall have the blessing of the covenant. Oh, this is a great excellency! It is a special part of the covenant that God makes with His people on their part. On His part, He will be a God to them.

What is it that God required in Micah 6:6–7? There you can see how God prizes walking with Him, that it's the great thing that God looks at. Whereas there were some who said, "Wherewith shall I come before the Lord, and bow myself before the High God? Shall I come before Him with burnt offerings? With calves of a year old? Will the Lord be pleased with thousands of rams, or with ten thousands of rivers of oil? Shall I give my firstborn for my transgression, the fruit of my body for the sin of my soul?" They were asking, "What shall I do to please God?" Mark the 8th verse: "He hath showed thee, O man, what is good: and what doth the Lord require of thee, but to do justly, and to love mercy, and to walk humbly with thy God?" It is as if He should say, "This is the great thing, to walk with your God, not only to exercise some particular grace of your justice and mercy but, in general, to walk with your God. Never tell Me of anything you would do for Me, but in the constant course of your life walk humbly with your God."

This was the comfort of Hezekiah, when the message of death came to him in Isaiah 38: "Remember, O Lord, how I have walked with Thee in truth, and with a perfect heart; he turned his face to the wall and wept." It was as if he should say, "Lord, it's true, there have been many infirmities in me; but,

Lord, I have walked before Thee in truth, and with a perfect heart. I come now, Lord, to challenge the good of the covenant, that Thou wouldst remember me according to the riches of Thy mercy; for, Lord, I have walked with Thee. Lord, was not that which Thou required of my father Abraham? Why, Lord, I have walked before Thee, and have been upright in some measure. Therefore, Lord, be an all-sufficient God to me. Lord, remember Thy covenant; be a God to me; be all in all to me because of this."

O my brethren! Is not this worth ten thousand thousand worlds, that the soul may be able to appeal to God that it has done that special thing which is required of us in the covenant? And so, upon that, it may have the assurance of God's performing His part of the covenant.

5. There is a blessed safety in walking with God. In Psalm 23:4, David was a man much exercised in walking with God: "Yea, though I walk through the valley of the shadow of death, I will fear no evil, for Thou art with me. Thy rod and Thy staff doth comfort me." That is to say, "I am walking with Thee, and therefore, though I walk in the shadow of death, I'll fear no evil." Is it not a blessed thing to be in safety always with God? In Psalm 138:7 David says, "Though I walk in the midst of trouble Thou wilt revive me; Thou shalt stretch forth Thine hand against the wrath of mine enemies; and Thy right hand shall save me."

No matter what the trouble is, God is with the soul. He who walks uprightly walks surely, says Proverbs 10:9, whereas it is said of the wicked that they walk upon a snare continually (Job 18:8). The ways of wickedness may seem to be pleasant and comfortable to you, but certainly you are on a snare and may be caught and undone forever. Though you may have escaped so far, you are in continual danger. Every step you take in the ways of sin you are upon a snare, and in danger of being caught to your eternal destruction. But he who walks uprightly walks surely, and this is a great excellency. I know I am in my way, for I am with God. A child does not fear whatever way it is in as long as he can see his father. Now the soul may know surely that it is in the right way if it is with God. It is safe whatever danger comes, for it is walking with God.

6. From walking with God, the soul comes to enjoy a holy boldness and holy familiarity with God. It may be that when the soul first comes to God, the presence of the great God strikes some fear, and there is some dread of the majesty of God. But when the soul gets used to conversing with Him, there is a holy familiarity and a holy boldness that the soul has with God. It has liberty to say anything to Him now; and this is the reason that some never knew what the spirit of prayer meant, and what the liberty of the soul in opening itself to God meant before. Yet when they have come to be acquainted with the ways of God, what liberty they have in their spirits to open their hearts to God, yea, they can open their hearts to God as one friend to another.

I remember it is said of Luther that, whenever he was praying, he could speak to God as his friend. Job 22:21: "Acquaint now thyself with Him, and be at peace." The soul comes to have an acquaintance with God, and, oh, what a phrase is this! What? Acquaint ourselves with God, that God should be our acquaintance? Aye, God is willing to be the acquaintance of the poorest Christian in the world. Poor men and women, servants, and others may be scorned by rich people; they account them fit only to sit with the dogs of the flock. Though they are godly people, yet they think it would be debasing to have any kind of acquaintance with them. But the infinite God, though He is so high that He humbles Himself to behold the very things that are done in heaven, does not mind being one of your acquaintances, to be the acquaintance of any who has any godliness in them. When we see a great man, a man of parts and honor, come to some poor man and shake him by the hand, we will say, "Look what a humble man he is, who will be this familiar with the lowest of all." Oh, acquaint yourself with God! This is the blessedness of walking with God: the soul comes to have a familiar conversation with God, and a holy boldness.

7. The seventh benefit or excellency there is in walking with God is this, the communication of God's secrets. He who walks with God shall come to know the mind of God. It's impossible for a man to take delight in walking with another without discovering secrets from him. There's never any true friendship where there is not a closeness of spirit; but where there is true friendship, they will take one another and walk together and open their hearts to each other. This is comfortable walking, indeed, and thus it is in walking with God. This is the blessing of it, that such souls have the secrets of God revealed to them. They come to know much of the mind of God. Though they are weak in their natural parts, yet they come to know much of God's mind because they are with God.

We read in Proverbs 13:20 that the Holy Ghost said, "He that walketh with wise men shall be wise." Then what shall he be who walks with God? Surely if there is wisdom to be learned from walking with wise men, then there is wisdom to be learned from walking with God. 'Tis from hence that men who are weak in parts have come to such an excellent knowledge in great mysteries of the gospel, and you wonder at it. You see a lowly servant, who only a while ago could understand nothing at all, yet now he understands the great mysteries of the gospel beyond the learning of many great scholars. How does this come to pass? He walks with the God of wisdom, and the God of wisdom delights to let Himself out to him, to open His heart to him. These men come to know the counsels of God because they walk with Him.

Those Christians who keep close to God in holy conversation with Him certainly come to know more of the mind of God than others do. Others who walk loosely know little of the great mysteries of the gospel. They may talk something of them, but they do not have spiritual insight into the great mysteries of the gospel as do those who walk with God.

8. The eighth benefit of walking with God is that such find favor in God's eyes for granting their petitions, for hearing them in their prayers. Psalm 37:4: "Delight thyself in the Lord, and He shall give thee the desire of thine heart." Walk with God and enjoy conversation and communion with Him, so as to delight yourself with Him, and He will give you your heart's desire. You will have what you would have.

I remember reading of a man who offered to give a great sum of money to have the liberty to whisper something in the king's ear every day. Why? Because by that he thought he would have many people coming to him to get his help for their petitions. If he could have that liberty, he could get enough that way. Now the soul that has the liberty of walking with God, what privilege does it have? What opportunities to present petitions to God? And the Lord delights in hearing them. If a king will admit a man to walk with him, surely such a man, whatever he presents, is likely to succeed.

You see a great deal of difference in a formal professor's prayer and the prayer of a godly man who walks with God. The difference in the prayers of these two is thusly, and I'll set it out by similitude. You have beggars, and they pray for alms, but they stand at the door. But if you have a special friend, an acquaintance who comes desiring a favor from you, the door is opened for him. You take him to the parlor and there he opens his mind to you. He has a great deal more privilege than the other. Both come to ask a favor of you, but one stands at the door and the other is let into the parlor and walks up and down there, and there opens his mind to you. This is the difference between a formal professor's prayers and the prayers of those who walk with God. Those who make only a mere profession of religion will pray as others do, but they are like beggars at the door. They do not see God's face all the while. It may be that they knock, but the door is not opened for them to come in.

A gracious heart that walks with God, however, does not only stand knocking at the door, but it is opened to him and he comes into the Presence Chamber and there God says, "What is your request, O soul?" If a man should hear his dear friend knocking at the door, he will open the door and take him into the best room that he has and say, "Tell me what it is you would have. I am not able to deny you." And this is the privilege of those who are gracious and holy, who walk with God. They have much privilege in prayer, much benefit that way, freedom with God, and assurance that God will grant their petitions.

9. This excellency is from walking with God: there must be a glory put upon the soul. Moses went up on the mount with God for forty days; and when he came down his face shone so that the people were not able to behold it. God appeared in a visible manner to him. Spiritually, the soul that is conversing with God forty days, yea, in the constant course of his life has such a beauty, a luster, a glory put upon it, that those who have enlightened consciences and are guilty are scarcely able to bear the sight of them. I appeal to you, when you have given liberty to some way of sin, and have come into the presence of those who have been godly and walked closely with God, has it not struck a terror in you? There is a glory and beauty on

those souls that walk close to God. They shine in the midst of a crooked and perverse generation. What's the glory of heaven but the reflection of God's presence? And in its measure, a gracious heart that walks closely with God has the glory of heaven upon it.

10. God's presence acts mightily on every grace, draws forth every grace, and I lay that down as another distinct head in the excellency of walking with God. It draws forth every grace; the graces of the Spirit of God are always kept in action. For example, fire will draw fire. The Lord, being of infinite holiness, draws forth all holiness when the heart is holy from being in the presence of God and walking with Him. This will put a mighty beauty on men; they have not only grace in their hearts, but it is active. And this is a great blessing, to have our graces activated, drawn forth, and enlarged. This is the benefit of walking with God.

11. The presence of God, and familiarity of the soul in walking with Him, will keep God's presence at death or judgment from being a terrible thing. Those who now walk with God and have much conversation with Him shall not find His presence terrible when they come to die. Yea, when Jesus Christ shall come in flaming fire to revenge Himself upon those who do not know Him, His presence shall not be terrible to them. Why? Because they have walked with Him all the days of their lives. Hosea 11:10: "They shall walk after the Lord, He shall roar like a lion." Mark how these two are joined together; wicked and ungodly men shall tremble at the roaring of a lion, but it shall not be terrible to the saints.

How much is it worth to have the terror of God taken away when He shall appear in death and judgment? My brethren, God appears at death and at the times of judgment ordinarily in another manner than He does in the time of prosperity. You see no terror in God's presence now, but beware of it when death is approaching. When wicked men lie upon their death-beds, how terrible is the presence of God to them then! But those who walk with God shall not find it so. When they die, then God appears to them. "Now I am going to stand before the great God to have my eternal state determined one way or the other. But what God is this? He is great indeed, but He is my Friend. I have had conversation with Him all the days of my life. And so, when I come to the judgment, here comes Jesus Christ with His thousands of angels in glory, but it is Christ who I have conversed with all the days of my life, this Christ has been my Friend." This will be the comfort of walking with God.

12. The end of the walk makes it blessed indeed. Oh, how blessed will that make it! It's a blessed thing to walk with God now, but when you come to the end of this walk you will find it blessed indeed! If a man comes to enjoy God, though he has to go through many difficulties to do so, he still has cause to bless God. If one were going to possess a kingdom, though the way there was hard and difficult, the end would make it comfort-able, because the end is to go and take a kingdom. But now, you who are walking with God have comfort in your walk, but the end of your walk will be glorious indeed. It is to possess a kingdom; it is to have the crown of glory set upon your heads. The communion that you have with God here is but the fore-runner of that glorious communion you shall enjoy with Him together with the saints and angels to all eternity.

And thus I have given you the headings, at least, of the excel-lency that there is in walking with God. Do not marvel that the Holy Ghost sets such a high commendation upon Enoch walk-ing with God, seeing that there is so much good in it. I confess that I had not thought to leave this head without applying it and warming it to your hearts, that you might so walk with God, that you might not lose the comfort, the blessing, and sweet excellency you have had opened to you in walking with God.

Let me say this, be in love with it. Know there is no such good in any other path. The devil deceives you and your hearts, and the world deceives you, if it promises any good thing in any other way than this. Oh, no; walking with God is the good of a Christian. It is his happiness, his glory, his commendation. Oh, that this might be recorded of you as it was of Enoch, "And Enoch walked with God."

CHAPTER SIX

Five Uses of Exhortation in Walking With God

USE 1. First, bless God that He will be pleased to walk thus with His poor creatures. Bless the Lord for His goodness to us. Happy are the angels that stand before the Lord. How happy are we, then, who may have this free conversation with God! What? We who were not only strangers, but enemies to God a while back are now able to walk with Him? Oh, it is a blessed thing! Let God be magnified for His goodness to us, even He who humbles Himself to behold the things that are done in heaven. Just look at the things that are done in heaven (Psalm 113); and yet He will condescend so far to His poor creatures here on earth as to walk with them.

Were we wholly freed from sin it would still be something; but we are not only lowly in ourselves but sinful, and yet God will walk with us. We have cause to bless God for this if we should see His face hereafter, though we never see Him in this world. But God not only grants that we will, after a wearisome and tedious pilgrimage here in this world, see His face, but that we should have so much conversation with Him here. Oh, magnified and blessed be the name of God forever!

USE 2. See what strangers most of the world is to this about which I am speaking. That of which I am speaking is a riddle to most men in the world. Walking with God is just an empty sound to most men. The greater part of the world walks after their own counsel. You will find several notable expressions in Scripture of the walk of sinners, of wicked men. They walk according to their own counsels; they walk after the flesh; they walk after their lusts. They walk after the course of this world; they walk in the vanity of their minds. They walk contrary to God; they walk according to men.

That brings us to this: the Holy Ghost condemns not only walking according to the course of the world but in Scripture to walk in the way of kings is condemned in 2 Chronicles 28:2. If one were going to follow the course of any man, you would think it might be most commendable to follow the king. But here is a charge against Ahaz, that he walked in the ways of the Kings of Israel. 2 Kings 17:8: "They walked in the statutes of the heathen." Here it is to walk as kings walk, to walk in the laws of kings. God would not have men walk any further in them than they are according to His own statutes. You are not to say, "It's the law, and I must walk according to the law." No, this is charged to walk according to the practice of kings, their laws being evil. There is another Scripture in 1 Kings 15:26: "He did evil in the sight of the Lord, and walked in the ways of his father, and in his sin wherewith he made Israel to sin." This is to walk in the way of great men, and that is condemned.

To walk in the ways of the laws of the places where we live, that is, to walk according to our fathers is condemned. And then to walk according to the common course of the world is condemned—yet this is the walk of sinners. Further, the Scripture says that wicked men walk in darkness, after their own imaginations and in the vanity of their minds. They walk in lies;

their hearts walk after the sight of their own eyes, and they walk after their covetousness. We might mention nearly twenty such expressions in Scripture; and all are the walks of sinners. But the ways of the saints are to walk with God. Those who walk in the ways of sinners, that is, in the vanity of their minds, according to the sight of their eyes, after their covetousness, after the flesh, and their lusts, and lasciviousness and vanity, shall have the end of their walk to be none other than destruction and misery.

USE 3. What vile hearts are ours that are so backward to walk with God, seeing God is pleased to admit His saints to walk with Him. Even those who are godly are to be rebuked from henceforth that they should be so backward to come in to walk with God. It is our glory; it is that which would make our lives comfortable; it would make this wilderness of ours to be a paradise. It would make our gardens to be Edens; it would make our houses to be churches, and make the church to be heaven to us—yet we are backward to this. Oh, that we would just consider this when we are in our walk and have vain thoughts!

Oh, the vanity and folly of the thoughts of men who are walking in their gardens or pleasant rooms! Who do you walk with all the while when you are walking in your galleries or parlors, your gardens, or when you are alone in the fields? Who are you parlaying with? Who are you conversing with? Are you not, many times, walking with the devil and making provision for the flesh? You should be walking with God. Are you not the saints of God? Does God offer Himself to walk and talk with you, and will you walk with the flesh and converse with the devil? Oh, what a vile and sinful thing this is! The Lord humble you for your sinful walks, you who are saints!

You have had some walks with God; why is it that you do not

walk more closely with God? You complain of your great business in the world, and that you have no time for communion with God; and yet when you are away from the world, and when you have time alone where you might converse with God, when you walk to and from the city, what communion do you have with God? How backward are our hearts to this, which is our happiness and our glory!

USE 4. Let us keep close to God in our walking with Him. We read that Peter saw Christ walking upon the water and wanted to leap out to walk with Him there. Though we are afflicted, it should be comfortable to walk with Christ. We read how idolators have their children pass through the fire to get to their idols. Oh, let us be willing to pass through any difficulties to get to God. The Lord is willing that we should communicate ourselves to Him, and He is willing to communicate Himself to us. The Lord would communicate word for word, promise for promise, embrace for embrace. If we would speak to Him, He would speak to us. If we would let our hearts out to Him, He would let His heart out to us. If we would promise to Him, He would promise to us.

The Lord often calls us to walk with Him. Sometimes close friends ask each other to walk with them, those who are close friends. Though they are busy they will lay aside their activity because their dear friends call out to them to walk. They take that much delight in it. Many times God, our Dear Friend, calls us, "Come, let us walk together." When God darts a heavenly thought into your minds, He calls you to walk with Him there, and would have you follow that thought. Following that heavenly thought is the answering of God's call to walk with Him. Consider this one thing, and do not refuse this. You do not know how your lives may be comforted this way, and how your hearts may be strengthened.

USE 5. If there is this much excellency in walking with God here, what will there be in heaven then? If our conversation with Him in this world is this sweet, oh, how sweet shall our conversation in heaven be with Him when we shall walk with Him in white! We shall have glorious garments indeed, and our souls will be fit to converse with God. Now, the truth is, we are very unfit to converse with the Lord because of our blindness and darkness. We do not know God. Let an ignorant man converse with a learned man. He gets little good from the discussion, for he is not able to put a question to him, nor able to understand what the man says, especially if he speaks with any depth of knowledge. So, many who are weak, when in conversation with those who are strong and godly, are not able to make conversation as others can. It's a great excellency for a man to be able to improve his conversation with men of ability and strength.

Alas! We are not able to improve our conversation with God here, but in heaven we shall be able to do so. We shall know as we are known; we shall understand God. If God communicates Himself, we shall be fit to receive all the beams of His glory that He shall be pleased to let out. Oh, that will be an excellent thing indeed, when we shall always be walking with God and conversing with Him continually. Bernard said of the gracious visitations of the Spirit of God to his soul, "How sweet, if it were not so little!" But then it shall be constant. We shall follow the Lamb wherever He goes, and walk with Him in white when He speaks.

The church cries out, "Oh, draw us, and we will run after Thee." The Spirit of God needs to draw us here, but then we shall have no such need of drawing, but we shall draw ourselves from the inclination of our own hearts. We shall be always walking and conversing with God. We shall have nothing else to do but to walk continually with the Lord. "I will walk in Thy truth; unite my heart to fear Thy name" (Psalm 86:11). It is an excellent Scripture. "I will walk in Thy truth," the prophet said. "Oh, unite my heart to the fear of Thy name!" It is as if he should say, "I find much sweetness and good in walking in Thy truth here. O Lord, unite my heart to the fear of Thy name! Lord, keep me always here." It is good to be here, as Peter said when Christ was transfigured in His glory. So when the soul is walking with God it says, "It is good to be here." When you come to heaven you shall always be with the Lord; and, therefore, from the excellency you find here, learn to long after heaven where you shall continually be with the Lord.

Take note of this one thing about the excellency of heaven, and only ones who have had much sweetness in their walk with God here will understand what I mean by this. Suppose that all those sweet manifestations of God to your soul here, and all the dartings of the Spirit of God, all those soul-ravishing joys you have had were all put together, that you had them all over again, but all at one instant. What a comfortable time it would be! At such a time some soul (who knows what the meaning of this point is) may say, "Oh, the sweet communion I had with God! I would give a world to have it again." Well, you had it once, but it was quickly gone; and you have had it a second and a third time. "Yea, many times when I have been with God I have had wonderful and gracious lettings out of my soul to God. Oh, that I had them again!"

Suppose you were to have now, in this quarter hour, all the comfort and joy that you have ever had in your life. Put all the good times together. What a comfortable quarter hour this would be! Now in heaven, to all eternity, you shall have infinitely more than that for millions of years, forever. Oh, what will heaven be! If I should set out heaven to a carnal man I would have to tell him of crowns of glory, and that there he shall see glorious sights. He shall be freed from all kinds of sorrows and there he shall have a kingdom. But if I were to set out heaven to a saint, I must tell him that he shall have communion with God and all those soul-ravishing comforts that he had in the presence of God in this world. He shall have them all together, and infinitely more than these. Oh, this is that which will make their souls long after heaven and set a prize on it!

CHAPTER SEVEN

Ten Distinct Evidences of a Man's Walking With God

QUESTION. Having had the excellency of walking with God set out to you, you might ask, "Who is it that walks with Him?" ANSWER. I shall set out to you the evidences of those men and women who walk with God.

1. One who walks with God is one who does not depend on sense or reason in the course of his life. One who is above the ways of sense and reason in his course of life has received a principle to go higher. Most men in the world walk according to sense. Therefore the Scripture says, "They walk according to the pleasure of their eyes." But now one who walks with God has his walk above sense and above reason. Though things of sense seem to go this way or that, quite cross to him, yea, though reason seems to go quite cross to him, still his heart is not in a hurry; but he has that which can quiet his heart even though sense and reason are quite contrary.

In 2 Corinthians 5:7 you see the walk of a godly man: "For we walk by faith and not by sight." Beyond our sight, either the sight of sense or the sight of reason, we walk by faith. This is a great point, a Christian walking by faith; and, therefore, I intend to speak to that by itself from this very text, God willing, in another treatise.

2. You shall find one who walks with God to be the same in private as he is in public. Whatever holiness appears in such a man before other people in his walking in the world, you will find it also in his private course. Why? Because he does not have to deal with man as much as with God in all his ways. When he has anything to do before others he walks with God, and when he is alone he is still the same man. See what David said in Psalm 101 about his walk in private with his family: "I will behave myself wisely in a perfect way. Oh, when wilt thou come unto me! I will walk within my house with a perfect heart." It is as if he should say, "I will not walk with a perfect heart only when I am abroad, but I will walk with a perfect heart within my house."

There are many people who, when they are abroad in the world, seem to be very strict in their way; but follow these men to their houses and you will see a great deal of difference. Many times you will find as much difference between the course of men when they are abroad and when they are at home as you will find in their clothes. You have many men and women who, when they go abroad, will be very neat, and though they have but little means, they will lay it upon their backs to look good abroad. Come to them in their families, however, and they do not care what clothes they wear there. It is just so in their lives; their lives have as much difference as their clothes. When they are abroad they put on a good face and seem to be very fair in their conduct; they speak good things, but at home they are contrary and perverse. Perhaps in their passion they will swear; they are profane and ungodly, and they vent their corruptions in a most ungodly manner.

Do you walk with God? If you had to deal with God, you

would be the same in your family as you are abroad, so that your wife, children, and servants might give as good a testimony of you as others do when you travel. Yes, and if you could retire with them into their closets you would find them the same there in any duties of religion. How outgoing some people are when they go abroad and join others, and how dead and dull they are when at home. Those who walk with God will be as spiritual in one place as in another. That is another evidence of one who walks with God: he is the same in private as in public.

3. A man who walks with God has a serious spirit. Walking with God will compose the spirits of men and women, will take off that looseness and vanity of spirit. Therefore, walking in the vanity of the mind is quite contrary to walking with God. In Ephesians 4:17 it is said of wicked men that they walk in the vanity of their minds. All wicked men walk in the vanity of their minds. Then all those who walk with God walk in the seriousness of their minds. They must have a seriousness of spirit in all their ways, for they have to deal with God. They do not take the liberty to run this way or that as others do. If a servant is walking with another servant, they can take the liberty to talk with anyone they please. But if a servant walks with his master or mistress, he must not take that liberty, but must go where they go.

Many who walk only with the creature take the liberty to run up and down as they please; but those who walk with God must have composed spirits and walk seriously. And though they walk seriously, yet they walk cheerfully. Consider that a Christian does not know the way of Christian rejoicing who does not know how to mix it with seriousness. Seneca was a heathen who could say, "Joy is a serious thing." There is a kind of seriousness in true joy, for the joy of a Christian is not light, it is a composed joy; it's serious.

First, a Christian with joy is able to command himself; he can let out his joy so far, and yet at his call he can command himself to the most spiritual duty in the world from his joy. He does not profusely let out his heart so that he cannot call it in again. Certainly you do not rejoice as a Christian if you cannot take your heart off of creature joys. God gives you liberty to be merry, but so as to have it under your control, so that you shall be able to call your heart from it to the most serious duty in the world.

Second, he cannot only command himself to holy duties in the midst of joy, but he finds himself all the more fit for holy duties by it. This is a serious joy if it is one I can control, and that makes me fit for that which is holy. Christians need to take heed of frothiness, slightness, and vanity; for certainly walking with God cannot help but make them serious. Those who are slight and vain do not converse with God, for God is a serious object, so that it's impossible that it would not work a seriousness in the spirits of men.

4. Those who walk with God walk in newness of life. This is not our natural walk, for walking with God is that which comes from a mighty converting that God gives to our spirits. Our walk is naturally with our lusts and with the devil and in the way to hell. But the one who walks with God walks in newness of life, as the Scripture says in Romans 6:4: "He walks according to the rule of the new creature." Galatians 6:16: "And as many as walk according to this rule, peace be on them and mercy."

What rule does the apostle mean here? I confess that, ordinarily, this refers to the walk according to the Scriptures. I grant that this is true, that the Word of God should be the rule of our walk and of our lives. Those who walk according to this rule shall have peace. But I do not think that is the meaning of this text. The scope is to be taken from the words of the former verse: "In Christ Jesus neither circumcision availeth anything, nor uncircumcision, but a new creature. And as many as walk according to this rule," that is, according to the rule of the new creature, not standing so much upon external things, either circumcision or uncircumcision, not standing so much upon outward duties, but the main thing to stand on is the walk of the new creature. Those who walk according to the rule of the new creature, those who act as a new creature in their walk, "peace be unto them." That's the fourth thing in the evidences of one who walks with God: he walks in newness of life, and so according to the rule of the new creature.

5. When he has to deal with the creature, he quickly passes through the creature to God. Though a man is acquainted with this mystery of godliness, walking with God, while he is in the world he must deal, as do other men, with the creatures. Yet he will not stay there, but will soon pass from the creatures to God. He may receive sweetness from the creatures as do others; but when he has received it, his heart is on God. Oh, the sweetness that is in God! Is the creature so sweet? How sweet is God, then? It is sweet to have companionship with men; how sweet is it to have companionship with God, then? Do you have comfort in your wife? What comfort is there then in the comforts of my husband, Jesus Christ? Is there comfort in a sweet habitation? Then what comfort is there in God, our habitation? He is not relying on the world or on the creature, but he is relying on God in all that he enjoys. Those who stick to things in the creature are not acquainted with the way of walking with God.

6. A man who walks with God loves to be withdrawn from the world. It's true that he must follow his occasions in the world, he does that in obedience to God; but unless he has his secluded time, he does not know how to live. When he is in

his vocation he walks with God there; he carries his heart in a heavenly way. There's a great deal of difference between walking with friends and walking alone—though it's true that while the saints of God live in the world they must have dealings with the men of the world. They have something of God there but, though they have something of God there, it is not as much as when they are alone with God. This is that which is exceedingly sweet and comfortable to them; and therefore, they have their secluded times of meditation and secluded times of prayer.

We read of Isaac, that he went out into the field to meditate, to pray; for sometimes in Scripture, prayer and meditation are taken for the same thing. "I'll pour forth my meditations to Thee," said David; that was his prayer. So, because they should be joined together, Isaac went out into the field to meditate. Those who walk with God, if they live in a house with no secluded rooms, go abroad and have some time to be alone by themselves; whereas other men do not know how to spend any secluded, withdrawn times. When they are alone, their minds wander this way or that, and they gaze after every feather that flies. It is a prison to them to be alone, and they wonder how men and women can shut themselves up alone. To them it must be a person's depression. O poor wretch! You do not know what walks they have. They are not alone all this time. They would not give up their times of seclusion for all your times of gaiety or show. You think that you have a great life if you have been abroad, and there feasted, and had good cheer, music, conversation, and laughter. They would loath to change their times of seclusion for the times of your greatest gaiety with your companions. One who walks with God loves some alone times as well as to be busy in the business of the world.

7. One who walks with God is careful to make his accounts

with God even. It is a special thing in walking with God to lie down and consider, "Are my accounts even with God? Is there anything amiss between my God and my soul? What has happened today between God and my soul?" For how can two walk together unless there is harmony, as the prophet said. Therefore they are very careful to maintain their harmony with God. Indeed, Jesus Christ, their great Reconciler, has first reconciled their souls to God, and so they come to walk with Him; but later, in the course of their lives, they must keep up their agreement with God and not be ensnared by the world in the corruptions of their own hearts. And men and women will be ensnared if they are not careful to keep their accounts even with God daily. They will ensnare their souls in the world and in the lusts of their own hearts until God and their souls come to be strangers, yea, until they are almost afraid to think of God.

Here is the reason why many people are reluctant to pray, reluctant to come to duties of communion with God. It is because they have not kept their accounts with God even but have gotten behind, and their hearts are entangled in the world and in their lusts. Now, the presence of God is terrible to them. Oh, poor wretch that you are! You are a Christian, and yet the presence of God is grievous to you? Your condition is sad, indeed! You should be glad when you think of God, "I was glad when they said, 'Come let us go up to the house of the Lord.'"

One who does not keep his accounts even with God finds his times of seclusion to be grievous indeed; he does not dare have times of retirement. Why? Because he does not keep his accounts with God even. But the soul that does keep even with God rejoices in those times when it is to go to God or think of God. It is a special part of walking with God to keep their accounts even. I beseech you to observe that, as it is an evidence, so it may be given as a rule to help you to walk with God.

Be careful to keep your accounts daily.

8. The more spiritual any truth, ordinance, or company is, the more the soul delights in it. When one who is used to God and converses with God meets with a truth that has much of God in it, how he closes with that truth! When he meets with an ordinance that has much of God in it, when he meets with company that has much of God, how his soul delights in it! This is suitable to the heart that converses much with God. The soul says, "I have had sweet talks with God; and when I come into the company of friends I see the very image of God in them—and how sweet and delightful they are to me." It is the same with truths and ordinances: the more spiritual they are, the more a man can delight in them. A carnal heart, however, that walks according to the flesh, in the way of the world, delights in truths that have some humanity in them, some solid discourses that show strength of reason or judgment. If there is any wit, rhetoric, or eloquence, he will take delight in that. But there is no delight in spiritual truths unless they are clothed with some human excellency. But the more spiritual anything is, the more delight those who are spiritual will take in it. As for ordinances, they are just dry meat to those who are carnal unless there is something external. Bring the ordinances in the plain simplicity of the gospel to them, where there is only the communion of saints sitting around a table, eating a piece of bread, and drinking a little wine, and they see no excellency there. But a gracious heart, the less of a man he sees in an ordinance and the more of God, the more he closes with them and takes delight in them. This is one who walks with God.

9. A man who walks with God is one who walks in all the commandments of God. He endeavors to walk in them before Him, and is blameless before men. In Luke 1:6, it is said of

Zacharias and Elizabeth, "They were both righteous before God, walking in all the commandments and ordinances of the Lord, blameless." This is walking with God, not only to walk in some things, but in all commandments and ordinances of God—and, not only this, but blameless before men, too. It's true, the chief work a man has is to converse with God, yet he is careful to be blameless before men because the honor of God has a great deal to do with being blameless before men. Zacharias and Elizabeth were walkers with God, and their lives are described as being agreeable to all the commands of God, that they walked blamelessly before men. Now as we go along apply this. Can you say, "Lord, Thou who knowest all things knowest that there is no command of Thine, nor any ordinance of Thine, that my soul has not closed with; and I desire to spend my life in them and to walk blamelessly before men"? There are a great many who speak of walking before God, and of the ordinances of God; and yet, when they come before men, they are careless and negligent. Hearken to what the Lord speaks to you this day. Certainly you never knew what it is to walk with God unless you walk blamelessly before men also.

10. See how the Scripture describes the walk of the saints with God. There are some particulars that I shall insist upon, wherein I shall open some Scriptures that describe the saint's walk with God.

First, their walk is a walk of humility, a very humble way. The heart that walks with God must be very humble in the presence of God. You know the verse in Micah 6: "He hath shown thee, O man, what He would have thee to do, to walk humbly with thy God." To walk humbly with your God is more than the offering of thousands of lambs or ten thousand rivers of oil. A proud man or woman never knows what it is to walk with God; but walking with God causes much humility. There's no other thing in the world that will humble the heart of a man as having conversation with God. Do you see a man, proud and haughty, high in his carriage? You may surely conclude that this man has little conversation with God. Job said, "I have heard of Thee by the hearing of the ear, but now have mine eyes seen Thee." What then? "I abhor myself in dust and ashes."

Second, another thing that the Scripture speaks of regarding the walk of a Christian with God is uprightness: "Walk before Me, and be upright." I could give you twenty Scriptures to show how uprightness is the walk of a Christian with God. I'll only give you one and that is in 3 John 3, where this is expressed by the words, "walking in the truth." Sometimes in the Old Testament it is expressed by the words, "walking in uprightness." That and "walking in the truth" are somewhat the same. "I rejoiced greatly," the apostle said, "when the brethren came and testified of the truth that is in thee, even as thou walkest in the truth." This surely has reference to walking according to the truth of the gospel, in the truth and sincerity of our hearts. "They testified of the truth that is in thee," that is, the word of the gospel prevailed in your heart and, because it prevailed in your heart, you walked in the strength and power of that truth, and according to that truth. This is walking with God.

It is no wonder that the soul of this man was in as good a condition as it was. For you find in the 2nd verse of this epistle a very strange expression of John's about Gaius. What does he say of him? "I wish above all things, that thou mayest prosper and be in health even as thy soul prospereth." It seems that this Gaius had a poor, weak, sickly body, but a very good soul. John said, "I wish that you may prosper as much as your soul prospers. Oh, that you had as good a body as you do a soul!" It's a very strange expression. That would be a curse to many of you, I'm afraid. But John could say about Gaius, "Oh, that this man, Gaius, had as good a body as he has a soul!" And how did he come to have his soul prosper? He walked in the truth and according to the truth. All that he did was in the truth and sincerity of his heart; hence his soul came to prosper. And those who have weak parts, if they walk in the truth their souls will prosper.

The third thing is walking in the fear of God; indeed, the two are very near to one another. So you have in Nehemiah 5:9: "Also I said it is not good that ye do, ought ye not to walk in the fear of our God?" And he gives as an argument: "Because of the reproach of the heathen." So may I say to all Christians who would profess themselves to be Christians and godly, ought you not to walk in the fear of our God? Whatever other men do, ought you not to walk in the fear of our God? That's the walk of a Christian: the fear of God is continually upon Him. And observe, we read in Acts 9 of the walk of the Christians in primitive times, upon which they came to grow up in the ways of godliness as they did. The 31st verse says, "Then had the churches rest throughout all Judea and Galilee, and Samaria, and were edified." And what then? "They walked in the fear of the Lord, and in the comfort of the Holy Ghost, and so came to be multiplied." It's an excellent Scripture. Would you be built up in godliness? Let the fear of God be upon you, and if you walk in the fear of God you will walk in the joy of the Holy Ghost.

OBJECTION: You will say, "Fear may hinder our joy."
ANSWER: No, but the way to have true joy in the Holy Ghost is to walk in the fear of God. Though you have a company of vain and wanton spirits that want nothing but gaiety and mirth, they cannot allow any kind of seriousness. But certainly their gaiety is only light and carnal. However, those who have the best joy in their hearts walk most in the fear of God. When I see a Christian

have the fear of God upon him in the whole course of his life, then he will have much of the comfort of the Holy Ghost.

Fourth, the comfort of the Holy Ghost is joined with the fear of God. If you see any who talk much of the joy they have, it is a light, carnal joy, unless the fear of God is upon them. Oh, it will be a means to convince others of the excellency of the ways of God when they shall see Christians walk in the fear of God. The text says, "They were multiplied." There were many who were convinced by it and joined with them, because they saw such a beauty and excellency in their way, walking in the fear of God and in the joy of the Holy Ghost. This was at a time when they had much rest.

It may be that when many people are in danger they seem to walk in the fear of God; but mark it, this was in a time when this people were freed from their danger; then they walked in the fear of the Lord and in the joy of the Holy Ghost. That was increased in them. This is the walk of the saints.

I shall mention two or three more things. The walk that they walk is above. The way of the saints is on high; it's a walk above the world. They keep themselves on high, aloft in a spiritual way. It's true, their hearts are humble before God, and yet they are on high, too. Though they do not look at themselves as worthy of the least crumb of bread, yet they look upon themselves as too good to be servants to the world or to their lusts. They look upon themselves as being set by God in too high a condition to be satisfied with all the world as their portion. Their hearts are lifted up on high to converse with the Most High God, and so they come to be delivered from the snares of death that are below. Also they endeavor to walk as Christ walked, as in 1 John 2:6: They walk as Christ Himself walked, those that walk with God. Who ever walked with God as Christ did? Whoever had that fellowship with the Father and the Son as Christ had? The saints labor to walk as Christ walked, to look upon Christ as the pattern of their lives. And so as Christ was anointed with the oil of joy and gladness above His fellows, so they come to have some of the ointment run down upon them. They come to have something of that communion that Jesus Christ had with the Father in the constant course of His life. Now the saints, laboring to walk as Christ walked, come to have communion with God. May the Lord bring you into this walk, and keep you in such a blessed walk as this.

CHAPTER EIGHT

Twelve Rules of Direction for Walking With God

What rules should be observed for a Christian's walking with God? You will say to me, "You have shown us that it is a most blessed thing to walk with God, and we are convinced of it, but what rules are given for it?"

RULE 1. Be sure that there is no way of sin in you. Take heed of giving way to any sin, especially any known sin, though it is a little one, though it is only a sin of omission. Giving way to any known sin will make the presence of God terrible, and will make all your duties empty. It will estrange God from your soul. There is more evil in it than you are aware of. You can have no communion with God while you are in a way of sin, especially if that sin is against light. The least sin that a Christian gives in to is like a thorn in a man's foot; but a great sin, and a sin against knowledge, is like a great gash in a man's foot. Now if a man has a thorn in his foot he cannot walk well; it will make him stop. If a man has a little gravel in his shoe he will not be able to walk a long way. He may walk a step or two, but not very long.

Now small sins are like gravel in the shoe or like a thorn

in the foot. But if you fall into a great sin, a sin against light, against conscience, that is like a great gash that one may cut with a hatchet or an axe. If a man has cut a great gash in his foot he will hardly be able to walk with any comfort. In the same way, when you fall into any great sin you need to go to the surgeon, you need to have salve applied to you to heal your soul, otherwise it will hinder your walk with God.

RULE 2. Labor to abstract your heart from earthly and sensual things as much as you can so that you may be spiritual. A drossy, earthly, sensual heart is unfit to have communion with God. God is a Spirit, and you must be spiritual in your conversation with Him. Take heed of mingling your hearts with creature comforts. You may make use of them, but do it in a spiritual way. Do not defile your heart with them; do not let your heart close with them as adequate objects of your desires or love. Take heed of being entangled, of being ensnared with any creature comforts.

A man cannot walk if he is trapped in a snare. When men fetter themselves in the world, and entangle themselves with an abundance of business and creature contentments, it mightily hinders their freedom in walking with God. When men's hearts sink down to the creature, they cannot walk with God for God is above. He is on high, the way of the wise is on high, and we must keep ourselves on high. Christians sometimes have good affections; their hearts are a little stirred up to things that are good; but at other times their hearts sink down to the world and to sensual, earthly contentments. They cannot walk freely with God. A man with one leg shorter than the other cannot walk evenly. So our affections are up and down; they sometimes are stirred up to heaven, and sometimes down to the world again. Some truths heave us upward and a drossy spirit sinks us downward. Our affections must be even; they must not be for heaven and earth together unless one is in subordination to the other. While we are on the earth, we are in heaven. We keep our hearts in subjection to spiritual things even when we are busy with earthly things. Then is a man's heart spiritual and separated from the earth, when he knows how to have comfort in God alone, when he knows how to make up all the lack of creature comforts in God Himself—that's a spiritual heart. No Christian can walk with God unless he attains to that pitch, to know how to make up all in God and use all in order for God.

RULE 3. If you would walk with God, evermore take Christ with you. God and the soul cannot walk together except with Christ: Christ, God and Man, that Mediator. By that I mean this: in all your conversation with God, have an eye to Christ; look unto God, the infinite, glorious First Being of all things, but do it through Christ, the Mediator. Otherwise God will not be rendered amiable, sweet, and lovely to you. Then God is rendered sweet and amiable, lovely to the soul, like a friend that the soul can be familiar with, when He is looked upon through Jesus Christ. Do you do all by Christ, by the strength of Christ, and offer up all your services to God through Christ? Those who are not acquainted with the mystery of the gospel in Christ know little of this walk with God.

OBJECTION: You will say, "But Enoch did not know much of Christ."
ANSWER: Oh, yes! Though it was long before Christ came, yet his eye was upon Christ; for in Hebrews 11:5 the apostle says that it was by faith that he walked with Him. It was all by faith. Now Christ is the object of faith, and so his eye was upon Christ. It was through faith. And I will give you one Scripture that will

show the use of eyeing Christ in walking with God. Exodus 25:21: Thou shalt put the Mercy Seat above the Ark, and in the Ark thou shalt put the testimony that I shall give thee; and there will I meet with thee, and I will commune with thee," that is, there at the Mercy Seat.

They were to come to the Ark and look to the Mercy Seat, and there God said He would meet with them and commune with them. Now what is the Mercy Seat but Jesus Christ? We must look upon God in Christ; and so God is rendered amiable, sweet, glorious, and lovely unto us in His Son. There God meets with His saints, and there He communes with them. Indeed, while we look upon God as He is in Himself, He is a consuming fire; and we cannot expect to commune with God there. Therefore, those who look upon God merely in a legal way look upon Him as One who exacts and requires such and such services and duties of them. They merely consider God as a Judge. If they do not perform such and such duties, they do not meet and commune with God. But those who look to the Mercy Seat look to Christ by faith when they have to deal with God in Christ. Oh, these meet with God; these commune with God. There's much sweet communion between God and their souls. They walk with God because God, through Christ, comes to be rendered gracious, lovely, sweet, amiable, and familiar to them.

RULE 4. Be careful to beautify the soul. Look to your spirit rather than to your outward actions in walking with God. God is a Spirit, and will be worshipped in spirit and truth. One who would walk with God must be careful of his spirit. Keep your heart with all diligence, for it is with your soul that God converses. Indeed, 'tis the proper sphere of a Christian to be busy about his heart, to be busy in the inward man. There's the sphere of a Christian. It's not so much the outward man, for if the heart is kept in a right frame, the outward man will be brought over of its own accord.

Be careful of your spirit, that is, of the thoughts of your mind. Take heed of allowing any uncleanness in your thoughts, for the soul converses with God in thoughts as well as we converse with men in words. How do you commune and converse with men but by speech? Therefore, God gives speech to men that they may converse with one another. What speech is to men, thoughts are to God. We converse much with God by our thoughts. Make conscience therefore of thoughts. Labor to cleanse your thoughts and, likewise, the affections of your heart and the stirrings of your heart; for God and your soul converse together. In the workings and stirrings of your heart, look to your spirit; and labor to beautify your soul with that which may make you amiable and lovely in the eyes of God. Then the Lord will delight to converse with you and walk with you.

If you were asked to walk with a man who was your superior, some chief in your parish, a gentleman, knight, or nobleman, you would labor as far as you were able to adorn yourselves with suitable clothing. You who profess yourselves to be Christians, God calls you every day to walk with Him; and if you expect to have communion with God, and that God should take delight in you, you must labor to beautify your souls, to dress yourselves with those things that may make you amiable in the eyes of God. Do not come dirty and filthy into the presence of God.

Now that which makes the soul amiable in the eyes of God is holiness; for it is the very image of God, and God delights to walk where He can see His own image. The more resplendent the image of God is in the soul, the more the Lord delights to walk with such a soul. Labor to make the behavior of your soul suitable to God. When I walk with one who is my superior, I must have a demeanor that is suitable to his presence; and, as was said before, to walk with God is to walk in the fear of God.

Take heed to your spirit; beautify your soul in that which can make you amiable and lovely in God's eyes, and carry yourself as is suitable to the presence of God. I shall only give you one Scripture about beautifying your soul. In Psalm 45, where it speaks of the church and the saints being brought into the presence of God, it says in the 13th verse, "The King's daughter (that is, the church) is all glorious within." (Many make great shows of religion without, but the King's daughter is all glorious within.) "Her clothing is of wrought gold." There are her ornaments; now mark what follows in the 14th verse: "She shall be brought unto the King in raiment of needlework." She shall be brought to the King, Jesus Christ, with garments of needlework. By that is meant the distinct graces of the Spirit of God that put a beauty on the soul. As there is a variety in needlework that brings a beauty to the work, so shall she be brought to the King. So you must have that which may make you amiable and lovely in the eyes of the King.

RULE 5. Take heed of halting. When you walk with Him you must not halt between two opinions, but give yourselves up fully to God. You must give yourselves wholly to Him in walking with Him. Do not have a distracted heart or a divided heart. "Why halt ye between two opinions," said the prophet. "If God be God, worship Him; if Baal, worship him." So, when the heart is not divided and is resolved in the way of God, that's the thing I mean here. If I cannot be happy here, I am content to be miserable here. The soul is resolved and does not halt in God's way when the soul knows that here is the way to happiness, though it seems contrary to flesh and blood. I know that there is happiness to be had in these ways; there is enough to bless my soul forever. And therefore, whatever becomes of me, I am resolved upon these ways. This is one who is fit to walk with God. He will not halt, but will tread straight steps in the ways of God. The apostle requires it of us in Hebrews 12:13: "Make straight paths for your feet, lest that which is lame be turned out of the way." Make straight paths; go on in a straight way; do not have the heart long after something else.

There are some who have some convictions of conscience, who have their hearts inclined to the ways of God, and are going on in some of the ways of God, yet they have longings of spirit after something else. But when the heart walks with God, it gives up itself wholly to Him and is resolved in these ways. You have had some good thoughts, but if your hearts are divided between God and the world you will be turned into an apostate in time. That which is lame will be turned out of the way; the ways of God will be tedious to you when you do not give yourselves wholly to them. This is the reason for the apostasy that there is in the world. Men seem to go on in God's ways, but they go on lamely because they do not give themselves wholly to the ways of God.

RULE 6. If you would walk with God, take heed of formality in all holy duties. Be laborious in holy duties; take pains with your hearts in them; labor for the power of godliness in holy duties. You must strive to get up to God in them. It would be well if, when we perform holy duties, we kept close to the duty itself. Few go so far. But it's one thing to keep close to the duty and another thing to keep close to God in the duty. We must labor not only to mind what we are doing, but to keep close to God in the duty, to find God in all duties that we perform, and in the use of all ordinances to take pains to find God there, and not to satisfy and quiet our hearts unless we find God in the duties that we are performing.

We have a notable Scripture for this in Exodus 20:24: "In all places where I record My name, I will come unto thee, and I will bless thee." That is, wherever there is any ordinance or any holy duty to be performed there is a recording of God's name. And, He says, "I will come unto thee, and there I will bless thee." If you would walk with God you must go where God is, and be in those places where God comes. Now the place where God walks is in His ordinances, in His worship; therefore you must be very spiritual in worship and sanctify the name of God there (according to that which we have treated at large in *Gospel Worship*). You must take pains there; stir up your hearts, and all that is within you to walk with God there, and not be satisfied unless you have something of God there. It's a notable speech of Bernard, "I never go from Thee without Thee." Whenever I come to any holy duty and leave it, I never leave it unless I have You with it. We must not be satisfied unless we meet with God in holy duties.

RULE 7. Take heed of secret declinings or sliding away from the paths of God into any bypaths. Those who profess their desires to walk with God will not forsake God and His ways in an open way. But if you are not watchful over your hearts, you will have them secretly decline away from the ways of God, from those paths wherein you have had communion with God heretofore. Oh, take heed of turning out of the paths of God, of any allurements from the flesh, of any temptations, and especially such temptations as are suitable to your corruptions. They will be alluring you to lead you out of the ways of God, and seem to promise ways of contentment to the flesh.

Take heed of any such thing; take heed of being allured through the deceitfulness of the flesh, as the apostle says in 2 Peter 2:18 where, speaking of false teachers, he says, "When they speak great swelling words of vanity, they allure through the lusts of the flesh, through much wantonness, those that were clean escaped from them who live in error." There were some who escaped from the ways of error, from sinful, ungodly ways, and really escaped. That is, in their kind they were not hypocrites, making show of one thing and doing another, but what they did, they did according to the light of their consciences. Yet it was not through the sanctifying, saving work of God, but through the strength of a natural conscience. So they were allured through the lusts of the flesh, through wantonness, by those who taught false doctrine; but they, together with their false doctrine, came to that which was suitable to the flesh. I beseech you to observe this. Some who have been walking with God and then met with these who come with fair shows, with that which is false, think that here is a fine, even, and smooth way in which their flesh can be content.

Observe it, there's no such way to allure those who have, by the power of the Word, escaped from the ways of sin in a great measure, no such way to allure them as to show them how they can make a profession of godliness and still have liberty to the flesh, too. Oh, may the Lord deliver young beginners from the wanton ones of our age! The wanton ones in our generation allure them through the lusts of the flesh and promise liberty to them, for the text says so: "While they promise them liberty they *themselves* are the servants of corruption." Mark that those who promise liberty, and bring such a doctrine of liberty to you, are themselves, in the meantime, the servants of corruption. Oh, take heed of declining to the ways of the flesh after you have seemed to begin in the spirit! What do you have to do with the way of Asher and the ways of Egypt?

You who previously seemed to converse with God and to walk with Him, what iniquity have you found with God? What evil have you found in the ways of God? Do you find them too difficult for you? It is through the baseness of your heart, because your heart is not changed and made suitable to that which is spiritual and holy.

Oh, that the Lord would be pleased to cause His angels to meet with some who are declining from His good and blessed ways! As we read in Genesis, the angel met Hagar when she was flying from Abraham's family, from the church of God, and said, "Hagar, Sarah's maid, from whence camest thou?" Do you come from Abraham's family? Are you going from there? And where do you think to find so much good as in Abraham's family where the presence of God is?

Oh, that God would meet with those who are declining from the good ways of God! O soul, where are you going? You who have had the Word working on your heart and seemed to be turned to the good ways of God, where are you going? Are these the ways that are like the former ways you seemed to walk in? Oh, what will be the end of the ways you are now in? Indeed, they give contentment unto the flesh more than the former ways, but do you think that the end of them will be peace? Oh, that there were a messenger from God to meet you in those ways in which you are walking, that you might say, as the church does in Hosea 2:7, "I will return to my first husband, for then it was better with me than it is now." I used to have more peace, comfort, and sweetness in conversing with God than I now find. I will return to those ways of God no matter how many loose professors scorn and deride them. Lord, I am sure that I found more sweetness in them then than now. I will return to them and labor to walk in them.

RULE 8. If you are declined, labor to keep a tenderness of

spirit so as to be sensible of the beginnings of declining. It's true, we have a great deal of corruption while we remain here in this world, and our hearts are quickly drawn from the ways of God. But if we could keep a spirit sensitive to the beginnings of declining, we might still keep our walk with God. If we just began to think to ourselves, as soon as we got just one step from God, "Where are we? What are we doing?" This would cause us to return and not go very far from God. For a man to go far from God is very dangerous; for then he begins to have many thoughts of despair. So many times he grows desperate in his course and gives himself up to excess to satisfy the lusts of the flesh with greediness. There are some men who are convinced that they are out of the way; and though they are convinced of it, they still go further and further from God.

You might ask how that can be possible. Once a man makes a profession of religion and departs from God, the devil follows him with despairing thoughts. He thinks that God will not receive him and accept him if he returns. Therefore he is resolved that he will satisfy himself to the fullest. I truly believe that this is the great reason why many apostates turn as notoriously wicked as they do. When you see a man who has been ardent in religion fall away, and not only that, but becomes a drunkard, a whoremaster, or a scorner, you may almost conclude that this is the ground of it. Though his conscience is convinced that he is out of the way, he is in a desperate manner to have his pleasure, because he thinks God has forsaken him and he has forsaken God. He will have his lusts, and that's all he has to satisfy himself with. Oh, take heed of getting far from God! Hearken to this, you who are far from righteousness as the Scripture speaks. It's a terrible thing to be gone far from God. Labor to keep your hearts watchful of the beginnings of declining and be tender and sensitive of them.

RULE 9. Labor to be spiritual in your solitary times. If you would walk with God, prize your solitary times much. Labor to be spiritual in them. Do not lose those times when you are alone, when there's none but God and you together. You who have much business in the world especially, alas, what little use do you make of your solitary times? When you are alone you don't know what to do. But a man who would walk with God needs to be careful to be very spiritual there. Now I am separated from the world; now I have to deal with God and my own soul. Oh, let me improve this and get advantage by this! Oh, do not let me be quiet until I get some conversation with God! Those Christians who are spiritual in their solitary times will be very spiritual when they come into company. When Moses was alone with God on the mountain and came down to the people, his face shone so that they were not able to bear it. Certainly, those that are alone with God and are spiritual will shine in holy conversation when they come down from the mountain, when they come to converse with others.

RULE 10. Let God's presence be more to you than all the world. Count it more attractive to your soul to be with God, and to have God's presence with you, than if you had the eye of all the world upon you. It would mightily compose the spirits of men and women if they had an aweful reverence of the presence of God, and counted it more than all the world besides. Therefore, do nothing in God's presence but what you would do in front of all the world, or what you may do without your conscience accusing you for it. Oh, look upon the presence of God as more than all the world to you!

RULE 11. Go on with a resolution in the performance of holy duties though you see nothing come of them for the present.

Though I do not have the comfort I wish, yet I am doing what duty I am commanded. I am still in God's way, and that should satisfy every gracious heart. Though I do not have the encouragements I wish, yet I am in God's way. Let me keep in that way of God.

RULE 12. Make good interpretations of all God's ways and dealings with you. This is a mighty help to us to keep on in the way of God and to walk with Him. If God comes in a way of affliction, make good interpretation of that affliction. Do not conclude that God appears like an enemy to you; that will discourage you in the ways of God. But look on God as intending good to you in everything, and that will help you to keep close to Him and walk close to Him in every condition. If God seems to go out of the way of prosperity and to come in the way of affliction, make good interpretations of it. Do not think, therefore, that God is leaving and forsaking you, but exercise faith. Believe that God intends as much good to you in that way as in any way whatsoever.

I ground this rule upon the passage in Hebrews 12. In the former part of the chapter, the apostle speaks of God's chastening of His people: "My son, despise not thou the chastening of the Lord, nor faint when thou art rebuked of Him; for whom the Lord loveth He chasteneth, and scourgeth every son whom He receiveth." Then in the 7th verse: "If ye endure chastening, then God dealeth with you as with sons, for what son is he whom the father chasteneth not? But if ye be without chastisements whereof all are partakers, then are ye bastards and not sons." He goes on in the point of chastisements in verses 9 through 11, speaking of nothing but chastisements. Now in the 12th verse, he draws a conclusion from this having laid this as a ground, that we are to look upon God as a father in chastisements: "Wherefore then lift up the hands which hang down, and the feeble knees, and make straight paths for your feet, lest that which is lame be turned out of the way."

It is as if he should say, "When you apprehend God in a way of wrath against you and not in a way of love, your knees will be feeble and you will not be able to go on with that cheerfulness, to walk with God in that hard way that He seems to be calling you to. But look at yourselves as sons, and look at God as intending good to you, so that by chastisements you may be made partakers of His holiness. Lift up the hands that hang down, and those feeble knees that were so weak that you were unable to walk with God. Those feeble knees will be strengthened if you make good interpretations of the ways of God and believe that the Lord intends good to you." This is also true of spiritual desertions. When God comes not only with outward afflictions, but with spiritual desertions afflicting even your souls, you must make good interpretations of them.

You might say, "That is when it's hardest to walk with God. Indeed, we might walk with God and keep on in communion with Him notwithstanding outward afflictions, but when the Lord seems to withdraw Himself both inwardly and outwardly, that's hard!" I will give you one notable Scripture about a child of God who followed hard after God, though God seemed to withdraw Himself from the soul. In Psalm 63, David was in the wilderness of Judah when Saul persecuted him. Saul persecuted David and followed him, and David was forced to hide in the wilderness and move from place to place. Yet mark his words: "O God, Thou art my God; (yet for all that) early will I seek Thee; my soul thirsteth for Thee, my flesh longeth for Thee in a dry and thirsty land where no water is." And then in the 8th verse, "My soul followeth hard after Thee." That is, "Though, Lord, Thou seemest to withdraw Thyself from me in regard to these outward administrations, still my soul follows hard after Thee."

In times of affliction, when God seems to withdraw Himself by His afflictions, our souls should still follow hard after God. Does God seem to go from us as if He would not walk with us? Run after Him! If a child's mother gets away from him, the child will cry and run after her. So it was with David. When the Lord seemed to be going away, David said that his soul followed hard after Him. This is an excellent frame of spirit, that the more the Lord seems to be gone from a Christian, the harder the soul follows after God. Nothing can satisfy such a man but God Himself; and, therefore, David says, "Lord, my soul thirsts for Thee in a dry land." He does not say "after water," but "after Thee." So, in any affliction, you can say this, "Lord, it is not so much the deliverance from my affliction that my soul thirsts for; but, Lord, Thou knowest that my soul thirsts for Thee! If the affliction is only made up in Thyself, that will be sufficient. I never find my soul following more earnestly after Thee than now in my time of affliction."

CHAPTER NINE

An Objection Concerning God's Hiding His Face

*I*f the Lord seems to withdraw Himself from the spirits of His servants, if it is a spiritual desertion, what rules should be given for one yet to walk with God in the time of spiritual desertion? I have several things to say to those from whom God has seemed to withdraw Himself.

OBJECTION. You will say, "You have told us of the excellency of walking with God and we count it the happiness of our lives to walk with Him, but God will not walk with me. He withdraws Himself from my soul so that I cannot see Him and He hides Himself from me."

ANSWER. To this I have several things to say. In the first place, be of good comfort. It's a good sign that you can be sensitive to His withdrawings when God has made you know what it is to walk with Him. There is a generation of people in the world that goes on in a slight way in the profession of religion. They do not know what it is to be sensitive to any of God's withdrawings from them. You never hear them complain of any such thing; they do not know what it means. Therefore, it's a good sign that you know what it is to walk with God because you are

254

sensitive to any of God's withdrawings from you.

Second, examine whether you have not shut God out sometimes when God has offered Himself to walk with you. Has God not sometimes offered Himself and even taken you by the hand to walk with you, yet you have not been free? Your mind has been on something else. Oh, be humbled before Him for all your unworthy dealings with Him, and for all your declinings from Him! Know that God calls you to this. There have been many wanderings of your spirit from God. Oh, that you could just say, in respect of your spiritual wanderings, what David said about his wanderings in Psalm 56:8: "Thou tellest my wanderings, put Thou my tears into Thy bottle, are they not in Thy book?" Oh, that Thou could just say so! Lord, there have been many wanderings of my spirit, but put my tears into Thy bottle. Suitable to my wanderings are my tears. Oh, it grieves me to the soul that I have ever grieved Thy spirit! When Thy spirit has taken me by the hand to walk with Thee, I have withdrawn myself, and, upon that, Thy spirit has been grieved. Oh, it grieves my soul! O Lord, Thou hast taken notice of my wanderings; take notice of my tears that are suitable!"

Third, it is better that God withdraws than that we withdraw. If God withdraws from you it is your affliction, but if you withdraw from God it is your sin. Sin is worse than affliction. It is better to bear any affliction, even spiritual afflictions, than to commit sin. You should labor to be sensitive to this, you who complain about God withdrawing from you, and that God will not walk with you. Be more sensitive of your own withdrawings as a greater evil than God's. It's true, God's withdrawing from me is a sore affliction, above any that ever befell me in this world; but my withdrawing from Him is a greater burden to me. And it may be that if God did not withdraw from you, you would withdraw from Him.

Many times God withdraws from His people to prevent them from withdrawing from Him. Mothers will withdraw from their children so that their children will not wander from them. This may be the very reason why God withdraws. He sees your heart begin to be loose, wanton, slight, and vain, and therefore hides Himself so that you may be awakened and sensible of the danger that you are in by withdrawing yourself from God, that you may cleave to Him all the more fully, that your soul may follow more after Him, that you may lift up your heart and cry more earnestly after God. But now if God is withdrawn and the soul is not sensitive enough to cry after Him, or if it should stop crying, then such a man is in a dangerous condition. Take heed of that; do not depart from the Lord; keep crying after Him in all His withdrawings.

Fourth, God's withdrawing of comfort is not always the withdrawing of His presence; you may err. You think that God is withdrawn. Why? Because He has withdrawn comfort. There may be a great mistake in this. God may withdraw comfort and not withdraw His presence. Take this as a certain rule and make much use of it when comforts are gone. Do not say, "When comforts are gone, the presence of God is gone." There may be as full and as gracious a presence of God when comforts are gone as there ever was. He may be present with His graces and support. Psalm 63:8: "My soul followeth hard after Thee. Thy right hand upholdeth me." Though He seems to be gone, God may be present to uphold and strengthen you.

The exercise of faith in the lack of comfort may have as much of God in it as all the comfort that you have ever had in all your life. Therefore, do not say that God's presence is gone because comforts are gone. The beams of the sun in the wintertime are not as effective as the influence of the sun behind a cloud in the summertime. Is the presence of the sun gone in the summer because there is a cloud between you and the sun? A child might think, "The sun is gone from the sky because there's a cloud." I know the sun is still there because I feel the influence of the sun. There's some heat in the day; there's light for me to do my work by, even though it does not have the same luster as before.

When the sun shines in the winter it shines bright; but there is not enough influence on the earth to make plants grow. So sometimes the beams of God's presence may be clouded to a Christian by reason of outward afflictions, and yet there may be more of God's presence than at another time when it shines in the beauty of comforts. I liken the shining of the comforts of a Christian to the shining of the sun in the winter that sometimes has no influence to sanctify the heart. In winter, the sun does not have the influence to sweeten the ground; but at other times, though the sun is clouded, it has the influence to make the ground fruitful. So, though God may not shine upon you with regard to comforts, yet He may shine in your soul and make you to increase and grow in goodness more than ever before.

Fifth, if you cannot see God's face, yet hearken and see if you can hear His voice, and follow that. Do you come to the Word and there hear His voice? Is not God pleased to speak to your soul out of His Word? If you go into your closet and cannot see His face as you would like to do, yet bless Him that you can hear His voice, and follow it. If a child gets lost from his father and begins to cry, the sound of his father's voice will quiet him down. So it is with the children of God. When they cannot see God's face they can still hear His voice. They cannot have those comforts from God as they sometimes have had, those sweet manifestations of the love of God shed abroad in their hearts, but when they come to the Word, they cannot help but hear their Father's voice. Perhaps these words are not as comforting to you as those that have come before, but are they not directing words, instructing words, enlightening words? This should support you for the present.

Sixth, all that I will say further is this, keep yourself in a waiting frame for God. Do not determine that because the Lord is gone He will be gone forever. Oh, no! Just keep on in the ways of God, waiting for Him. Resolve that though God leaves you, still you will not leave the path in which God was before this. Keep the path where you used to meet with God, for you shall meet with Him again. It's better to keep the path, the ordinary highway of God, for you are more likely to meet with God there than if you go out of the way.

I'll give you a Scripture or two and then conclude. This first is Psalm 101:2: "I will behave myself wisely in a perfect way. Oh, when wilt Thou come unto me?" I quote that for this purpose, the resolution of David to behave himself wisely in a perfect way, together with his panting after the presence of God. "Oh, when wilt Thou come unto me?" It is as if he should say, "Lord, Thou art absent from me now; but, Lord, I will not go out of the way wherein I was wont to find Thee. Oh, when wilt Thou come? I will not determine that I shall never see Thee in this way as heretofore I have done. No, but I hope I shall afterwards meet Thee."

And then note Psalm 119:8: "I will keep Thy statutes." Then what? "Oh, forsake me not utterly." It seems that the Lord, in David's mind, had forsaken him for the present. But what was David's resolution? "God has forsaken me, so I'll forsake Him?" Oh, no, but "I'll keep Thy statutes. Oh, leave me not utterly!"

Keep on in the ways of God. Go on in His way; wait for the presence of God until He comes and conclude this: "Surely

He will come." Do not be like children who see the sun going down and conclude that the sun is gone, never to come again. Though God seems to withdraw the light of His face from you, do not conclude, "Well, I shall never have those comforts from God, in communion with God, in walking with God, as once I used to have." Do not say this, but go on and keep in the ways of God. Wait upon Him and look up towards Him; and so you may come to have as much communion, sweetness, and joy in God as you ever had in all your life. And now know that God calls for the work of faith in such times as these are. Now God calls you to walk by faith and not by sense.

FINIS